Ac

MW01121323

"David Hunt knows how to be a friend. I can personally attest to this, having had the privilege and joy of being his friend and colleague for many years. More importantly, in *To Be a Friend*, he shows us all how we can be better friends by attending to the dual challenges of relationships, knowing oneself and attending to the other. In Part Two of the book, through carefully and sensitively created exercises organized around opening up, letting go, and accepting, he guides us in translating that attention into actions that can bring vitality and fulfillment to our friendships.

David Hunt brings to this work the accumulated wisdom of his long and distinguished career as a psychologist leavened by his own personal experiences in the conduct of friendship workshops and as he says 'following my own advice.' And good advice it is. Take in the uplifting humanity of this work and rededicate yourself to the practice of friendship by following his guided exercises. You will be rewarded ... and so will your friends!"

— *David A. Kolb, professor of Organizational Behavior,*
Case Western Reserve University

"Friendship in our lives is a gift. It is rooted in years of experience from someone who has nurtured friendship in both professional and personal settings. This book is filled with practical suggestions that can help us be a better friend to ourselves and others. What I especially liked about this book were the many examples of how to be a friend that Dave Hunt offers from his own life. What emerges is the lived experience of friendship that is deeply authentic."

— *Jack Miller, professor,*
OISE/University of Toronto

"To be a friend is a critically important book, mainly because it isn't a book and what's more important than friendship? This combination handbook/workshop guide engages the reader to genuinely engage, first with oneself in gaining self-knowledge through reflective practise, then with others. This well-written effort is filled with poignant examples and stories and it feels as though you are actually in a workshop with David Hunt supporting and guiding you along the way."

— *Charles E. Pascal, executive director of the*
Atkinson Charitable Foundation

To Be a Friend

The Key to
Friendship in
Our Lives

DAVID E. HUNT

DUNDURN PRESS
TORONTO

Copy Editor: Nicole Chaplin
Design: Jesse Hooper
Printer: Webcom

Library and Archives Canada Cataloguing in Publication

Hunt, David E., 1925-
        To be a friend : the key to friendship in our lives / David E. Hunt.

Issued also in an electronic format.
ISBN 978-1-55488-751-4

        1. Friendship. I. Title.

BF575.F66H85 2010   177'.62   C2010-902680-2

1   2   3   4   5   14   13   12   11   10

We acknowledge the support of the **Canada Council for the Arts** and the **Ontario
Arts Council** for our publishing program. We also acknowledge the financial support
of the **Government of Canada** through the **Canada Book Fund** and **Livres Canada
Books**, and the **Government of Ontario** through the **Ontario Book Publishers
Tax Credit program**, and the **Ontario Media Development Corporation**.

Care has been taken to trace the ownership of copyright material used in this book.
The author and the publisher welcome any information enabling them to rectify
any references or credits in subsequent editions.

                                                        J. Kirk Howard, President

Printed and bound in Canada.
www.dundurn.com

Dundurn Press	Gazelle Book Services Limited	Dundurn Press
3 Church Street, Suite 500	White Cross Mills	2250 Military Road
Toronto, Ontario,	High Town, Lancaster,	Tonawanda, NY
Canada	England	U.S.A.
M5E 1M2	LA1 4XS	14150

Mixed Sources
Product group from well-managed
forests, and other controlled sources
www.fsc.org Cert no. SW-COC-002358
© 1996 Forest Stewardship Council

In memory of my mother,
Lucille Ellis Hunt,
who taught me how to be a friend

Contents

Preface

The flow of friendship in our lives is as vital for our physical health and well-being as the flow of blood in our arteries. We often fail to recognize that our need for friendship is as strong as our other basic needs for food, water, and air. This is especially true in today's pressure-packed, 24/7 world when we need friendship to sustain us in these stressful times. However, many people are so busy doing more and more, faster and faster, that they have no time for friendship.

My book is a wake-up call for everyone, including myself, to pay attention to friendship and to encourage it in our lives by learning how to be a friend. To do so, I offer a version of my workshop here. As a psychologist, I have held many personal development workshops during the past thirty years, which provide the foundation for this workshop. It is also based on my on my personal experience of learning to be a friend, which has reaffirmed the old saying: to have a friend, I need to be a friend.

You begin the workshop by learning to be friends with yourself through specific activities. In the next section you will learn how to be a friend to others, and in the final section you learn to strengthen your existing friendships. You learn through recalling your own experience in order to bring out your personal beliefs about friendship. Knowing your own beliefs allows you to develop you personal style of friendship. There are many ways to be a friend, and by engaging in the workshop you're enabled to apply your personal beliefs and find your own way to being a friend.

Engaging in these workshop activities calls for making a major shift from that of a passive reader to an active participant, which is not easy. Each activity includes an example from an earlier participant or from my personal experience. I also include an introductory section describing how I developed the workshop over the past several years.

I conclude by describing my experiences learning to be a friend, including my failures as well as the welcome flow of friendship when I succeed. Offering friendship to another person is the first step to receiving friendship, but it is not a guarantee. Whether or not the offer of friendship is reciprocated, I always feel more alive through expressing friendship. Offering our friendship is the key to opening our human potential, to become what we may be. I discovered this unexpected benefit while trying to strengthen my friendships, by helping my friends reach their potential. I was surprised to realize that when I focused on helping my friends reach their hearts' desires, I opened new possibilities for my own development. I hope my book will help you enjoy many of these benefits in your life as you learn to be a friend.

Introduction

It's friendship, friendship,
Just a perfect blendship,
When other friendships have been forgot,
Ours will still be hot.
— COLE PORTER

OUR NEED FOR FRIENDSHIP

I am glad that I finally awoke to my strong need for friendship in time to write this book, but I have to wonder why it took so long for me to recognize that nothing is more important in my life than friendship. When I take the time to recall how much the support and love from my family and friends means in everything I do, I immediately recognize its significance. For many years I took friendship for granted, failing to recognize how much I needed its refreshing flow in my life. Now that I have begun to realize how much it means, I want everyone, including myself, to become aware of the importance and meaning of friendship in our lives. I hope that discovering its personal meaning will become the foundation for our learning to be a friend.

My initial wake-up call regarding my need for friendship came a few years ago when I suffered a serious heart attack. There is nothing like going into cardiac arrest to put you in touch with your mortality and your good fortune at being alive to enjoy friendship. My experiences in a cardiac support group also bolstered my realization about the importance of friendship.

Shortly after leaving the hospital, I joined an Open Your Heart support group, which followed the program for cardiac survivors developed by cardiologist Dean Ornish. While similar to other heart-healthy programs in offering suggestions for diet, exercise, and stress management, the Open Your Heart program has a distinctive emphasis on learning to open our hearts. To do so, we open up to our own feelings and those of others in order to connect with each other, and as I came to realize, to learn to be friends.

The Open Your Heart program is based on Dr. Ornish's belief that any blockage of the flow of love and friendship in our lives is as serious a risk factor in heart disease as the blockage of blood flow in our arteries. He supports this radical belief with experimental evidence on reversing heart disease.

Increasing evidence from my own research and from other scientific studies reaffirms my belief that love and intimacy are among the most powerful factors in health and well-being.

As implied by the title of Ornish's second book *Love and Survival*, our need for love and friendship is vitally important:

> The desire for love and intimacy is a basic human need as fundamental as eating, breathing, or sleeping — and the consequences of ignoring that need are just as dire.

His strong belief in our need for love and friendship was the touchstone for organizing our support group activities as we strove to open our hearts. Each week we devoted one hour to focusing on opening to our feelings, to the feelings of others, and to friendship.

As a result of my experience in the Open Your Heart group, I came to realize that the need for friendship is very similar to other basic needs for food, water, and air. Just as my health depends on my receiving sufficient and appropriate food, so too does my well-being depend on my receiving sufficient and appropriate friendship. Since I usually take both needs for granted, it is only when I am cut off from food or friendship that I become aware of their importance. When cut off from friendship, the feeling of emptiness is as intense as the empty feeling in my stomach when I am hungry; in both cases, being deprived gets my attention. It is true that friendship deprivation is not as life threatening as starvation, but loss of friendship takes its toll through inner misery.

Have you heard the call to recognize your need for friendship? We need friendship more than ever in today's hectic world, yet many people feel they no longer have time nor the mental space to give and receive friendship. In recent surveys, people report that they have less time for friendship today than in the past, and that they have fewer friends. It's ironic that many feel cut off from friendship in the current Age of Technology, which promised increased opportunities for leisure and friendship. Technology has spawned many means for electronic connection — voice mail, cellphones, email, Facebook, and BlackBerrys — which may temporarily pacify people's social cravings, but these electronic connections cannot satisfy their deep yearning for a direct, personal connection: the basic need for friendship. For example, I often see people hurrying along on the sidewalk chattering incessantly on their cellphones. They are electronically connected, it's true, but unconsciously they long for something more to fill their empty hearts.

When we finally become aware of our need for friends, we often only think about getting love and support from others without recognizing the equal importance of giving friendship in return: to be a friend. Friendship involves both giving and receiving in a magical interplay which Vanier calls "the to-and-fro of love." It is through our spontaneous giving and receiving that we feel the warm flow of affection between friends. We need to give friendship to receive it, or as often been said, you need to be a friend to have a friend. This book will help you learn to be a friend.

LEARNING TO BE A FRIEND

In order to learn to be a friend, I invite you to actively participate in the workshop exercises in Part Two of this book. You will learn to be a friend by recognizing your own personal beliefs about friendship and actively applying them to your daily life. Taking part in the workshop activities takes more time, energy, and commitment than simply reading about how to be a friend, but it is absolutely essential. It will ensure that you get the most out of the experiences, and lean to be the best friend possible.

Offering workshop activities is my way of communicating about friendship. I have learned a great deal through my own active attempts to learn to be a friend, and I hope that through your engagement in the workshop activities, you will take these lessons forward in your actions.

Let me describe my plan for the book.

The book is in three parts: Part One tells the story of how I developed this workshop through the major themes such as "Beginning with Myself" and "Honouring the Mystery." Each theme discusses at least one author whose ideas have inspired me and how I have incorporated their ideas into my own. Part Two is the workshop itself, consisting of sixteen exercises. Part Three describes my experience learning to be a friend with different people and in different circumstances. You may choose to read the parts in a different order. Some may choose to jump right into the workshop, while others may prefer to read Part One first to find out the how and why of the workshop activities. Before moving on to Part One, I very briefly describe the importance of the key features of learning to be a friend: your personal beliefs and your private language.

PERSONAL BELIEFS

It is through our daily experiences that we become aware of our own personal beliefs, as well as our private language for expressing our beliefs. You may not realize how much you know about friendship, but each of us holds unique personal beliefs about friendship that guide our daily actions. You have developed your beliefs about friendship through thousands of interactions over the years with family members, friends, and acquaintances. The first step in the workshop is to become fully aware of these beliefs, as these are the foundation for learning to be a friend. Many workshop exercises invite you to recall your past experiences in order to discover your underlying beliefs. For example, recalling a positive friendship experience helps identify your ideal understanding of being a friend. You may also become aware of your beliefs through negative experiences by focusing on what was missing in these experiences.

PRIVATE LANGUAGE

We possess distinctive ways of expressing our beliefs through our inner language or self-talk. Like personal beliefs, we are often unaware of our inner self-talk, but it is essential to become aware of how we express our beliefs in our own terms, how we make them our own. Let's use the example of the Golden Rule of Friendship to illustrate the importance of making it your own.

The Golden Rule of Friendship instructs you as follows: let me be a friend to others as I would have them be a friend to me. The Golden Rule offers a specific guide for applying the idea that you need to be a friend to have a friend. However, following the Golden Rule of Friendship requires you to make it your own by translating it into your own private language. You need to identify your personal meaning for "as I would have them be friends with me." One of the workshop exercises is specifically aimed at making you think about how you would like to be treated as a friend. By recalling what it was like to be completely accepted by a friend, for example, you bring out your response to the Golden Rule instruction, "As I would have them be a friend." Through recalling your experience, you might identify the central feature as having received the complete and unqualified attention of your friend. If so, your application of the Golden Rule would be to try to give your undivided attention to your companion when offering your friendship.

You need to take one more step in order to make a specific application of the Golden Rule in your daily life: you need to make it your own. You need to become aware of how you actually express your belief in giving complete attention in your own private language. You might simply say, "Pay attention: I want to really know this person." For me, I often say to myself, "Let my ego go," as my private language guide for my offering my friendship.

This example of the Golden Rule applies to all other forms of advice: you must make them your own in order for them to be helpful. They are presented *out* there and you must bring them *in* here for them to make a difference. From *outside-in* to *inside-out*, these workshop activities are designed to help you become aware of your personal beliefs and to express them in your own private language so that you can apply them in your daily life.

Part One:

How the Workshop Developed

This workshop is a culmination of my thirty years experience offering workshops on personal and professional renewal, as well as my own experience of personal renewal. These exercises represent a summary of my personal beliefs about friendship and life. This section gives a brief description of how my personal beliefs have developed. My experience of learning to be a friend has been of great personal and practical value. I hope that through describing how my beliefs developed I can encourage you to discover your own personal beliefs. Although my beliefs are neatly organized into six themes, the development of these beliefs was neither logical nor organized. For example, in several cases, there was a long interval between the event that influenced my belief and my appreciation of its importance.

I have organized the story of the development of my beliefs in terms of the following major themes:

- Beginning with Myself
- Opening My Heart
- Connecting with Others
- Learning from Experience
- Taking Action
- Honouring the Mystery

Included within the descriptions of each theme are my personal and professional experience, as well as some of the ideas which have influenced me greatly.

BEGINNING WITH MYSELF

The foundation of all my work as a psychologist is captured in the title of my 1987 book, *Beginning with Ourselves*. In this book, I described how workshop participants discovered the value of beginning with themselves through their personal beliefs. I called my approach "inside-out," to emphasize the importance of focusing on our inner resources, as well as to distinguish it from "outside-in" influences, which are often distractions from our inner reflection. We need to be open to both inner and outer influences, but it is import to begin with ourselves to establish a foundation upon which we can interpret these external influences. Going "inside-out" helps you discover your inner resources and build your confidence. That is why the present workshop begins with a focus on yourself in order to learn to be a friend with yourself.

GEORGE KELLY'S IDEA OF "MAN AS SCIENTIST"

It was long ago and far away, as the story goes. I was a graduate student at Ohio State University when I first learned the notion of beginning with ourselves through my professor, George Kelly. I began my training in clinical psychology at the same time as Kelly was developing his theory of personal constructs, which he published a few years later. His theory was based on the belief that as we go through life, we form impressions of what is going on within and around us. From these, we construct our personal views of ourselves and others, which guide our actions. One person's constructs may be quite simple, consisting only of good versus bad; others may possess much more complex belief systems. In either case, their personal constructs serve as interpretive filters for understanding their experience, directing their actions. Kelly believed that we are like scientists in that each of us is continually experimenting with our personal constructs to determine their value in guiding our lives. He saw man as scientist.

In his clinical psychology course, Kelly recommended that we begin our work with clients by appreciating their personal constructs. (Note the similarity of his recommendation to the Exercise 13 on appreciating your friend's wishes). In addition to my experience as a student in his class, I was fortunate to work on his research team. During research team meetings I became intrigued with Kelly's ideas, which led to my master's thesis research into a method for bringing out subjects' personal constructs. My research revealed enormous variation in how people view their world, and create personal contracts, which planted the seed for my book, *Beginning with Ourselves*. It took twenty-five years, though, for me recognized its value in my own life. This happened when I translated Kelly's idea of man as scientist into my own terms: every person is a psychologist.

EVERY PERSON IS A PSYCHOLOGIST

My version of George Kelly's idea that every man is a scientist, "every person is a psychologist," does not mean that anyone can offer psychotherapy or administer psychological tests. Rather, it means that each of us possesses our own personal theory about human affairs. We are like psychologists as we formulate theories about how we develop, how we communicate, as well as what we desire and fear. To assert that every person is a psychologist might be slightly hyperbolic, but I wanted to draw attention to the important point that each of us possesses our own theory and expertise about human affairs.

It was while working with a group of teachers during the mid-1970s that I came to rediscover the idea that every person possesses an inner knowledge that guides their actions. By writing books and developing models on matching your teaching approach to your student's learning style, I played the role of expert for how to apply these ideas. In talking with the teachers, the moment of truth arrived! I finally realized that these experienced teachers possessed their own theories and models of matching that were informing their actions. They did not realize this because they were too busy teaching to fully describe their matching models. It was humbling to realize that some of the teachers not only knew as much as I did about matching models, but some knew even more. This insight was an indelible reminder that each of us is our own expert in human affairs, and led to my book *Teachers Are Psychologists Too*. It was also the basis for my workshops and courses for experienced practitioners, aimed at bringing out and sharing their personal theories and beliefs. I revised and updated my master's thesis approach to develop a series of exercises entitled, "How To Be Your Own Best Theorist," which became the foundation for my early workshops. In addition, I developed a graduate course, which offered time and opportunity for experienced practitioners to explore their personal beliefs. And, of course, the present workshop is based on my belief that every person has his or her theory of human affairs and friendship.

INFLUENCE OF EARLIER WORKSHOPS

During the past thirty years, I have worked with thousands of workshop participants. Many of my workshops were also offered as graduate courses. Two of my graduate courses, Practitioners' Experienced Knowledge and Renewing Yourself, were essentially thirty-six-hour workshops in personal development. On the non-academic side, I offered workshops on personal and professional renewal in a variety of formats: one day, two day, and one week.

Participants were mainly experienced practitioners in the helping professions: teachers, counsellors, nurses, social workers, day care workers, and trainers. They came to the workshops for a variety of reasons: some were experiencing burnout, others felt disconnected, and all of them wanted to enrich their lives. As they found the courage to trust both themselves and others, they were able to open up and share, which in turn increased their self-confidence. Here is how one participant described its value:

> A resurgent sense of confidence in my own experience … a sense that my ideas, feelings, and beliefs are useful and valid, and do not have to be validated by experts.

I learned a great deal from working with and observing how participants strove to bring out their inner beliefs and apply them in their daily lives. Many participants were initially skeptical about the value of opening to their inner lives, but when they were able to trust my suggestions, most of them discovered the practical value in the process. By taking responsibility for themselves, to become the best they might be, provided practical evidence to support my long-standing belief in our human potential and our possibilities for positive change. In sum, I believe that we can always make a choice and that doing so is the key to reading our potential.

Many of the activities and exercises in the present workshop are based on my experience and observations in these earlier workshops. For example, the phrase "becoming friends with yourself" comes from a comment in a participant's description of the effects of the workshop: "I really know more than I thought, and the knowledge comes from self. I have learned to become friends with myself."

I began my earlier workshops with the general aim of helping participants open up to themselves, but I soon discovered that many participants were unable to open up because of inner obstacles blocking the way. They might be so preoccupied with past events that they could not open to the present or it might be that worries about the future blocked the way. Some participants found an overly harsh inner critic prevented their opening up. To help them deal with these obstacles, I developed exercises for Letting Go, similar to Exercise 5 in the present workshop.

OPENING MY HEART

My experience in the Open Your Heart program had a profound influence in my personal life and health, as well as a major source of my awakening to the essential value of friendship.

DEAN ORNISH'S OPEN YOUR HEART PROGRAM

Dean Ornish is a cardiologist and medical researcher, whose fervent belief in love and friendship is mirrored in the title of his book, *Love and Survival*:

> I have found that perhaps the most powerful intervention — and the most meaningful for me and for most of the people with whom I work, including staff and patients — is the healing power of love and intimacy.

His belief that being cut off from love and friendship — being alienated from others — is a major risk factor for heart health was the galvanizing force for developing the Open Your Heart program. His program was similar to other heart-healthy programs in emphasizing diet, exercise, and stress management. However, its distinctive feature was the inclusion of weekly support group meetings during which participants learned to open their hearts by expressing their feelings and listening to those of others in the group. Open your heart means opening yourself to the flow of love and friendship by allowing your feelings to flow.

When we are able to open our hearts at all levels — anatomically, emotionally, and spiritually—we can live every moment in fullness.

* * *

As a medical researcher, Ornish evaluated his Open Your Heart program by recording its effect on the heart-disease patients who took part in the program for more than a year. His careful observations of their heart health revealed remarkable positive effects, which he wrote about in his book, *Reversing Heart Disease*. Patients who followed his medical prescription for large doses of love and friendship enjoyed remarkable positive results, in most cases reversing their heart disease.

His revolutionary assertion about the negative effects of blocking of the flow of love, which would have been quickly dismissed earlier by the medical establishment, was strongly supported by Ornish's claim that "... increasing scientific evidence from my own research and from the studies of others that causes me to believe that love and intimacy are among the most powerful factors in health and illness."

The scientific evidence of reversing heart disease was sufficiently convincing that several insurance companies agreed to include participation in a week-long seminar of Open Your Hear as a legitimate and reimbursable treatment for heart disease.

My Experience in an Open Your Heart Support Group

Ironically, I suffered a heart attack while trying to improve the health of my heart. It happened while I was volunteering in a university research project studying the effect of aerobic exercise on cardiovascular functioning. After I passed the initial screening, I was assigned to a training program, which involved exercising three times a week on a stationary bicycle at a prescribed heart rate. During the sixth week of training, I experienced chest pain and, shortly afterward, suffered a serious heart attack. The cause was not the typical blockage or clot, but a muscle spasm brought on by the excessively high rate of exercise. The damage to the heart muscle was serious and irreversible.

It was a wake-up call to my mortality, especially when I went into cardiac arrest in the ICU, giving new meaning to the old song "My Heart Stood Still." Shortly after being discharged from the hospital, I heard about a new support group for heart patients. I became a founding member of the first Open Your Heart support group in Toronto.

Our group followed Ornish's four suggestions: diet, exercise, stress management, and group support. However, it was up to us to develop the specific details of our program. We began with five members (later growing to ten), and we developed a three-hour program, which we followed every Tuesday evening for almost ten years. In the first hour, we discussed our experience with diet and exercise as well as any information about recent research reports. For the second hour, we arranged for a yoga teacher to lead us in heart-healthy yoga exercises, intended primarily for stress management, but also for opening our hearts.

In the third and most important hour, we honoured the name of the program by opening our hearts, first to ourselves and then to one another. We tried to follow Ornish's suggestions to discuss our feelings with the class. By expressing our feelings and by listening to one another, we learned the language of the heart: to speak and listen from the heart. One of our group members called the third hour of our meetings an "oasis," while another dubbed it "our tree house," both images conveying the special climate of trust we developed. It is hardly surprising that through several hundred hours together, we became friends. Also, as one member observed, "Nobody croaked."

Perhaps the most distinctive feature of our group was that we rotated leadership among all group members. In contrast to other Open Your Heart groups, which were led by a professional, each one of us took our turn as leader. Since some members were new to the leadership role, we devoted time to discussing and learning the role of the leader, which also helped us open our hearts. It was more than worth the time and effort because, in looking back, it is clear that sharing leadership responsibility was a critical factor in sustaining the weekly commitment over the ten years.

I am very grateful to my friends from the support group for their trust and openness. My ten-year participation not only sustained the health of my heart, but also provided an opportunity for me to learn a great deal about opening my heart to friendship. It confirmed the importance of beginning with myself, as we first tried to express our own feelings before we listened to and empathically responded to one another. I grew to appreciate the enormous individual variation in how people express their feelings, as well as how they respond to others. I also learned that it is often difficult to open my heart, and that being patient and gentle with myself are valuable qualities.

CONNECTING WITH OTHERS

When I look back at my work as a psychologist, it seems that most of my activities and ideas were unwittingly leading me to the ultimate goal of learning to be a friend.

This section describes how my earlier activities contributed to my understanding of friendship and to the exercises in the present workshop. I will show how my earlier experiences have influenced my present view of connecting with others by describing an important influence in each of the past five decades.

My first influence came in the 1950s when I first read the introduction to Kluckhohn and Murray's 1948 book on personality, *Personality in Nature, Society, and Culture*:

> Every person is like every other person in some ways,
> Every person is like some other persons in some ways,
> Every person is like no other person in some ways.

These three lines are the foundation for Connecting with Others. They express the importance of accepting both how we are alike and how we are different: connecting as accepting our similarities and differences. In the 1970s, I first charted the three basic features of the present workshop — Self, Other, and Relationship — by describing them as the "New Three *R*'s: Reflexivity, Responsiveness, and Reciprocity": connecting as people in relation to one another. In the 1980s I learned the difficulties of establishing a culture of friendship through a research project aimed at creating classroom climates in which students were more closely connected and accepting: connecting as mutual adaptation. In 1992, I published the second volume in my Inside-Out series, *The Renewal of Personal Energy*, which emphasized the value of opening and sharing with others as an antidote to professional burnout and a means of personal renewal: connection as renewal. Finally, in this new century, I read *Vanier's Becoming Human* which gave me connection as a communion of hearts.

Connecting as Accepting our Similarities and Differences (1950s)

I repeat these three lines to emphasize their importance, and ask you to stop for a moment and take in their meaning:

> Every person is like every other person in some ways,

> Every person is like some other persons in
> some ways,
> Every person is like no other person in some
> ways.

These lines have had many different meanings for me over the years. In my first efforts as a psychologist, I focused on the second line by creating categories of similarity, such as personality types, learning styles, or developmental stages. When I began my personal reflection, I began to consider the third line which is not as easy to follow as it sounds. I am surprised to admit that it has been only recently that I have really thought about the first line; yet it may be the most important feature in connecting with others.

The three lines are expressed in abstract, outside-in terms, and I find it helpful to restate them in personal inside-out terms:

1. How am I like every other person?
2. How am I like some other persons?
3. How am I like no other persons?

Addressing these three questions has been very helpful in increasing my self-awareness, which in turn helps me connect with and accept others. When I acknowledged that my life was often guided by my personal desires and deepest fears, I was able to answer the first question by realizing that this was true for everyone. Each of us has our own desires and fears; the same is true for our foibles and foolishness. Realizing these universal personal characteristics helped me accept others. I also found it helpful to translate the three lines in terms of the other person to become more aware of our similarities and differences:

1. How is he or she like every other person?
2. How is he or she like some other persons?
3. How is he or she like no other persons?

Considering these three questions for myself and the other may seem excessively systematic, bordering on paralysis through analysis, but they contain the basic issues to be considered. I certainly do not go through a checklist of these three questions each time I meet a person, but they provide a helpful reminder for me to focus on the basic question: how am I similar to and different from this person?

CONNECTING AS ADAPTABILITY (1960s)

The 1960s offered many opportunities for an applied psychologist like myself, as the War on Poverty spawned many federal programs such as Job Corps, Teacher Corps, and the Peace Corps, among others. My experience developing programs for assessing and training Peace Corps volunteers in effective communication was an early example of connecting through awareness of the other's viewpoint and adapting one's communication accordingly. One exercise consisted of a role-playing situation in which the volunteer met with a South American immigrant who needed to learn about the balance of powers in the U.S. federal government to pass the citizenship examination. The volunteer was given relevant information and told that he or she could communicate in any way they wished during a specific time period. Meanwhile, the role player was trained to give cues of misunderstanding. Before describing what happened during these communication sessions, I need to remind you that this was the balance of power as seen about forty years ago.

I was astonished at the variation in the ways with which volunteers attempted to communicate. On the one hand, there were those who spent considerable time getting to know the immigrant in order to understand his viewpoint before attempting to communicate. Volunteers who took this approach adapted their communication according to their impression of how the immigrant could understand the complex concepts. In doing so, they emphasized the idea of balance of concrete objects such as balancing dishes on a tray, instead of focusing on the abstract ideas of the executive, legislative, and judicial branches of government. On the other hand, there were those who treated the assignment as an opportunity to deliver a lecture in Political Science 101 — "In the beginning the founding fathers, etc..." — which they continued despite the immigrant saying they did not understand.

I tried to capture this enormous variation in communication technique by describing the basic skills of effective communication as "reading" and "flexing." "Reading" consists of paying close attention to the person in order to identify a channel open for communication; "flexing" involves adapting one's approach to the listener's channel or viewpoint. Although I did not use the words, it is clear that reading and flexing are important skills in learning to be a friend. This is connecting as adaptability

CONNECTING AS PERSONS-IN-RELATION (1970S)

When I reviewed the development of my ideas of Self, Other, and Relationship, which serve to organize this workshop, I was struck by how long it took me to incorporate an idea. I must have known about these three features thirty years ago, because it was in 1979 that I published a paper that expressed these three features in more abstract terms. The paper was entitled "The New Three *R*'s: Reflexivity, Responsiveness, and Reciprocity," which translated as follows:

THE NEW THREE *R*'S	TRANSLATION
Reflexivity	Focus on Self
Responsiveness	Focus on Other
Reciprocity	Focus on Relationship

The New Three *R*'s made no appreciable effect on the field or on my work at the time. Perhaps the moral is that expressing ideas in alliterative abstractions is unlikely to have any significant effect. However, given the passage of time, I later applied the New Three *R*'s in my role as thesis supervisor. I translated the New Three *R*'s to guide my students in their planning and research of their doctoral theses with these recommendations:

THE NEW THREE *R*'S	TRANSLATION
Reflexivity in Research	Interview Yourself
Responsiveness in Research	Listen to the Participant
Reciprocity in Research	Negotiate Participation

My recommendations were based on the researchers' acceptance of the participants as people who, like themselves, were guided by their personal desires. The researchers needed to consider how to combine the intentions of the participant with their desire as researcher to engage their participation. Just as in the case of friendship, they needed to negotiate their mutual intentions so that each was respected and accepted.

Identifying the three categories of Self, Other, and Relationship allowed me to clearly focus my attention on each of these features in the workshop. It allows me to shift from me to you to us. The following quote from a workshop participant is a clear example of the value of connecting with others:

Making new connections with others is how I grow and change as a person. This requires the suspension of my personal agenda in exchange for a relational one. Relationships begin and grow when both persons are present in the experience together. It is then that we can journey together.

CONNECTING AS MUTUAL ADAPTATION (1980S)

The next influence on this workshop came from a research project in the 1980s, the aim of which was to initiate a climate of mutual respect and support in several grade eight classrooms. We proposed creating this kind of climate by training students in listening skills that they could transfer to their regular classroom activities. It is no surprise that it was difficult, if not impossible, to change the culture of the classroom; but more to the present point, I realize in looking back that listening-skills training should have begun by showing the students how to make space for the other person.

We conducted the research by training the students individually through a repeat-and-reply exercise. This exercise is aimed at slowing down the pace of conversation, so that listeners will attend more closely to the what is being said. The rules of repeat and reply are that you must listen to your partner and then repeat what you have heard to your partner's satisfaction before replying. If you have not listened or cannot repeat accurately, you cannot reply. Students quickly realized that they needed to pay attention, which is the major skill in listening. After about six weeks of listening training, the students applied what they learned in their regular classroom activities by using the repeat and reply rules when they answered questions.

The training went fairly well, but I was in for a surprise when the students returned to their regular classroom activities. When the teacher asked a question, she also instructed the students to repeat what the first student said before they could reply. After the first student offered an answer to the teacher's question, the next student would invariably try to answer the question without repeating what the first student had said. When the teacher reminded him or her to repeat and reply, the second student could not believe that he or she was supposed to actually listen to another student: what the students learned in listening training did not transfer to the classroom.

There were probably many reasons why our training failed to transfer, but in retrospect I believe that one reason was that we did not emphasize that the students need to first make mental space for the other person before they took in what they were saying. The training effects melted away as the students reverted to their longstanding, classroom habits, in which they race to be the first to answer each question. Classroom activities are often based on competition, so it's not imperative that each student knows what the others have said. Since listening to other students will not be on any final examination, it takes much more than a few weeks of listening training to change competition to cooperation in the classroom setting.

CONNECTING AS RENEWAL (1990S)

My 1992 book, *The Renewal of Personal Energy*, was based on workshops I conducted with many experienced professionals in the helping professions: teachers, nurses, counsellors, and social workers. Because many participants were dealing with professional burnout, these workshops, and the renewal book, were devoted to preventing and alleviating this burnout. This simple theme — that a powerful antidote to burnout is to open up and share with others — is supported by the experience of workshop participants. Their positive experiences came from engaging in what I called "sharing as co-creation" to distinguish it from sharing as simply show-and-tell. Sharing as co-creation was based on several qualities: openness, goodwill, respect, non-judgmental approach, and trust. Participants practised sharing as co-creation by listening and accepting their partner in the spirit of sharing. They found the experience of accepting and being accepted enormously helpful, and for many it was the first step toward recovering their energy and their confidence.

Several years later, and a little wiser, I realized the central role of friendship in the renewal of personal energy. For example, the qualities defining sharing as co-creation were identical to those associated with friendship: openness, goodwill, respect, a non-judgmental approach, and trust. The message in my renewal book was to open to friendship and love, yet these words never appear in the book. In hindsight I would now entitle my 1992 book: *Friendship: The Key to Personal Renewal.*

CONNECTION AS EMPATHY (2000S)

In our Open Your Heart support group, we tried to practise empathy by focusing on other people's feelings as we listened. It was through these weekly efforts at empathy that I discovered the specific meaning of empathy, and its essential importance in our friendship connections. Ornish emphasized empathy when he created Open Your Heart, but it remained an abstract ideal until I made it my own through trying to practise empathy.

Empathy has many meanings, but my personal meaning is simple: to focus my attention completely on the other person while letting go of my concerns. I try to understand and feel what the person is experiencing in their current circumstances, while I am not concerned with my own feelings. This means that when I respond to another person's experiences, I resist both the urge to give advice, as well as the temptation to describe my similar experience. Through my experience of trying to respond with empathy in our support group and observing the attempts of other group members, I saw that we all had strong tendencies to respond with one of the following responses:

"Why don't you try to do such and such … that always works for me"

OR
"I know how you feel … that happened to me and I felt like so and so"

Both of these responses focus on me rather than on the other person and reduce my expression of pure concern with how they feel. Of course, there may be times when giving advice is appropriate, such as if the other person requests it, but uninvited advice is often simply a way of avoiding the person's feelings. When I recall my similar experience, it might help me appreciate the other person's feelings as long as it is only a brief avenue away from my focus on the other, and not a long story of my experience.

Simple as it seems, empathy often calls for nothing more than focusing on the other person, and trying to feel what that person feels. It is through such direct attempts to know the other's experience that friendship flourishes.

JEAN VANIER'S IDEAS ON THE "COMMUNION OF HEARTS"

Finally, it was in reading Vanier's inspiring *Becoming Human* that my ideas about connecting with others and opening my heart were fused:

> The heart is never "successful." It does not want power, honour, privilege, or efficiency; it seeks personal relationships, a communion of hearts, which is the to-and-fro of love.

This opening of the heart implies vulner-ability and the unveiling of our needs and weaknesses. The heart gives and receives, but above all it gives.

Vanier's heartfelt words make a fitting conclu-sion to this theme: Connection as communion of hearts.

LEARNING FROM EXPERIENCE

I believe that we can best understand friendship through our personal experience. That is why I have described friendship from my own experience, and invite you to do the same through participating in the workshop exercises throughout the book. We not only learn through our experience, but the knowl-edge we gain forms an interpretive filter through which we communicate. We communicate more effectively by sharing our experiential knowledge than through written abstractions, which is why I use my own experiences to illustrate my beliefs about friendship.

Since we learn through experience, our expe-rienced knowledge is firmly connected to these specific situations. When I learn something from my personal experience, it is as if the knowledge I acquire were wrapped in an invisible layer of that specific experience. My knowledge of the importance of making space for another person, for instance, is wrapped in my specific experience of observing the failure of listening training that did not include making space. This is the basis for many of the exercises in the workshop that invite you to unwrap your own experiences to reveal your knowledge. For example, when you look at your experiences of being completely accepted, it reveals some of your basic beliefs about friendship.

Of course it's also important to look at other people's ideas. Here, I have found David Kolb's Experiential Learning Cycle to be enormously valuable. However, just as was true in the case of George Kelly's ideas, I have translated Kolb's ideas to make them my own. This theme describes Kolb's ideas, my translated versions, and a few examples of how I apply my belief through accepting the primacy of experience.

DAVID KOLB'S EXPERIENTIAL LEARNING CYCLE

I first discovered David Kolb's ideas from his 1984 book, *Experiential Learning*, which featured his Experiential Learning Cycle. We first met in the 1980s, when we became acquainted through exchanging workshops, Kolb offering one here in Toronto and I offering several in Cleveland. This arrangement has been mutually beneficial in our separate efforts to understand experiential learning and knowledge. I have found that Kolb's most valuable influence by far has been his experiential learning cycle. Here is the cycle and my translation:

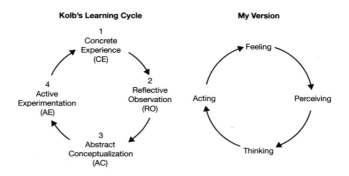

I especially like that the cycle begins with experience, which I translated as the experience of feelings. The cycle is the basis for several of the exercises that involve recalling past experiences. In Exercise 3, for example, you go through the cycle by first reliving the experience while focusing on your feelings, then reflecting to identify the highlights, next analyzing the reason for why this happened, and finally developing an action guide based on your analysis. I was surprised to realize after beginning to use the Three *A*'s of Attention, Awareness, and Action, that this sequence is very much like the cycle sequence from Reflective Observation to Abstract Conceptualization to Active Experimentation.

In addition to its vital role in developing these exercises, I have adapted and used the cycle for many different purposes, including a framework for identifying learning styles that extend Kolb's learning style inventory, a model for creative problem solving, and even a whimsical introduction to the cycle as a "wave," an exercise I will outline below.

COMMUNICATING THROUGH EXPERIENCE

In addition to offering workshops, I have often delivered conference keynote addresses. Since these types of addresses are a one-way means of transmitting information, I began to include within them mini-workshops in which I invite members of the audience to actively bring out their own experienced knowledge. Conference organizers did not always agree with my approach, but when they did, the results affirmed my belief in communicating through experience. On one occasion, I used my mini-workshop approach to communicate about learning styles with an audience of 800 participants. Rather than relying on a slide presentation, I asked audience members to actively recall their own personal learning experiences, both positive and negative, in order to form an impression of their learning style. I invited them to share their impressions with a partner, and opened the floor to questions and comments about their experience. Audience members were surprised by my request for participation, but almost all found it valuable. I will always remember the comment from the person who introduced me to the group, who said in a wistful voice, "It must be wonderful to be able to do what you believe in."

I hasten to add that I realize the transmission model of a PowerPoint presentation might be appropriate when communicating about complex technical topics; however, I don't think it is the method of choice when the topic is human affairs, such as learning style and friendship.

PRACTITIONERS' EXPERIENCED KNOWLEDGE

One of my most successful applications of learning through experience was in a graduate course I first offered twenty years ago, called Practitioners' Experienced Knowledge. It was designed for experienced practitioners in the helping professions — teachers, counsellors, nurses, social workers, daycare workers, and trainers — and offered a thirty-six-hour opportunity for them to bring out and share their experiences. I cannot take full credit for the course's success: my role was primarily to convince them that what they knew was worthwhile and then to get out of the way as they brought out and shared their knowledge.

Most graduate courses are designed so that the teacher transmits knowledge to the student; my role revresal in this course turned out to be not only atypical, but very popular. I taught over forty sections of this course, and there were almost always waiting lists. It was through this course that I first developed the introduction to the Experiential Learning Cycle. Rather than showing the Kolb diagram with a slide projector, I thought it deserved an introduction in its own terms, through the students' experience. Therefore, I introduced it with Exercise 3 in the workshop, which you will discover later, going through the sequence of feelings, reflections, analysis, and action in relation to their specific experience. On concluding the exercise, I showed the Kolb diagram. It was an example of beginning inside-out to understand outside-in.

Following this, I used a second and more whimsical activity called the Experiential Learning Cycle as Wave. Practitioners were seated in a circle and divided into four groups: a feeling group at the top of the circle, a perceiving group on the right side, a thinking group on the bottom, and an acting group on the left side. At my signal, the feeling group stood, waved their hands, and announced "Feelings," followed by the perceiving group which waved and announced "Perceiving," then the thinking group, and the acting group while continuing the wave. It was light-hearted, but it also conveyed the movement and flow of the cycle through their own bodily movements. Their experience of feeling the cycle's flow in their bodies helped them sense the flow in the exercise, which moved from recalling to highlighting to analyzing to planning.

In teaching this course, I also learned a general principle, which I applied in other circumstances: always begin with the students' experience. I often forget this principle, but when I remember it, the results are always positive.

TAKING ACTION

Actions speak louder than words. This is a reminder that in friendship, as in life, it is my actions that count. Yet despite its critical importance, I have been very slow to acknowledge its vital role in my personal life and in my work.

Until recently, I emphasized only awareness in both my workshops and my own efforts at development. Of course, awareness is necessary, but its importance is the result of the foundation is provides for my actions. Part of my overemphasis on awareness came from my work in academia, where thought reigns supreme. However, when I considered my own failure to take action, I realized that my resistance came from a deeper reason: taking action on my beliefs often requires changing my actions, which in turn calls for giving up long-standing habits. In short, taking action requires me to take responsibility and make a choice to do something.

Yet, it is through taking action that I extend the thread of trust, which is the foundation for developing friendships. As you begin to trust my actions, our ties of friendship strengthen. It is also through my actions in living my beliefs that I gradually develop confidence in myself. And it is through my taking action that I extend my initial awareness. Actions not only speak louder than words, they also extend our understanding.

LIVE THE QUESTION

Rilke's advice to a young poet provides the foundation for my theme that actions do speak louder than words.

... be patient toward all that is unsolved in your heart and try to love the questions themselves, like locked rooms and like books that are written in a very foreign tongue. Do not now seek the answers, which cannot be given to you because you would not be able to live them. And the point is to live everything. *Live the question now*. Perhaps, you will then gradually, without noticing it, live along some distant day into the answer.

In this profound paragraph packed with ideas on the importance of taking action, Rilke's first piece of advice — to be patient — is not only the most valuable, but also the most difficult, as I have found in trying to *live the question*. Following his advice to be patient means much more than to do nothing, to not respond. How often have you heard, "I'm just not a patient person," as if being patient were an impossibly difficult proposition. To be patient is difficult, but it is not impossible. When someone says "I'm just not a patient person," the unspoken message is "I need to know what is happening right now and why." This obsessive need to know applies to a wide variety of events from the simple ones, such as why an elevator or subway is slow, to larger ones, such as why my efforts don't produce results. If I am completely preoccupied with trying to answer the question rather than living it, as Rilke suggests, my impatience becomes an increasing source of anxiety, which further fills my mind.

To be patient, therefore, I need to let go of my insistence on knowing everything immediately and accept my not knowing, which is not an easy task. Admitting I do not know is difficult because of pressures to know as much as possible in both my personal life and in my professional work, which calls for expert knowledge. As I continue my efforts to *live the question*, my most important influence has been to follow the guide: Honour the Mystery. I will describe how this helped me live my life in more detail in the next section.

I love the phrase, "live everything," with its feeling of freedom and wholeness. It reminds me that living the question does not mean putting my head down and forging on. Rather, it means going ahead with full presence through awareness of my senses, feelings, and body, as well as everything that is occurring outside of me. To live everything is a fusion of action and awareness, but it goes beyond them to a deeper level of my complete trust in myself. *Living the question* offers the possibilities of future answers, but it does not guarantee them. I am pleased when my continuing actions bring new insights, but that is not my purpose in staying the course. I continue to try to live the question because I believe it may encourage friendship to flow in my life.

TAKING ACTION IN A GRADUATE COURSE

The renewal course for my grad students was based on my 1992 book *The Renewal of Personal Energy*, and focused specifically on the five qualities I deemed most important for the renewal process: Respect, Openness, Optimism, Patience, and Humour. In each case, students first delved into their personal understanding of each quality through several exercises focused on their experience with the quality, their image of the quality, and their meaning of the quality using a meaning map. In the first case, each student developed his or her personal meaning of Respect. Students were surprised at my next assignment, in which I invited them to discover Respect in their daily lives.

The assignment for the following week was to keep notes as they tried to live with respect and to observe the occurrence of respect or its absence in the action of others. During the class following this assignment, I was amazed at the level of discussion, which was more meaningful than earlier discussions based solely on the abstract meaning of respect. All of the students found it difficult to show respect, and were enormously relieved to learn that everyone had difficulty taking action. They reported an unfortunately high incidence of disrespect, especially in TV shows and movies. By taking action, their understanding of both the specific meaning of respect and the more general meaning of the phrase "Actions speak louder than words" was increased.

My focus on the importance of taking action came late in my teaching career, and I could not help but wonder how different my earlier courses might have been had I infused them with this lesson. It is almost as if there were another world with its own language of meaning — the world of action — and it is only by entering this world that we will find its meaning.

HONOURING THE MYSTERY

I have been developing this theme for many years in my struggle to accept the unknowable aspects of life, but only recently have I found the words to describe my struggle. I discovered the phrase, "Honour the Mystery," from Thomas Moore's thoughtful book *Soul Mates: Honoring the Mystery of Interpersonal Relations*.

In what follows, I will describe the influence of both Thomas Moore's ideas of honouring the mystery and John O'Donohue's chapter, "The Mystery of Friendship," in his 1997 book *Anam Cara*. Both of these authors helped me appreciate the meaning of honouring the mystery of friendship. Far from simply letting in the dark side, following this theme enhances my experience and opens new possibilities for friendship. Honouring the mystery also offers welcome relief in my work as a psychologist — and as a friend — by relieving my burden of understanding everything about how and why persons live their lives.

THOMAS MOORE'S IDEAS OF "HONOURING THE MYSTERY OF INTERPERSONAL RELATIONSHIPS"

Moore begins by acknowledging that the theme is beyond words: "I present relationships here ... as a mystery ..., knowing that it is always a mistake to talk authoritatively about mysteries." He continues, "Relationships, I believe are truly sacred ... in that they call upon infinite and mysterious depth in ourselves, in our communities, and in the very nature of things."

Following these initial comments, Moore gets more specific in describing the mystery of relationships, and in doing so, offers a succinct summary of the basic ideas in this workshop:

> A soulful relationship offers two difficult challenges: one, to know oneself... and two, to get to know the deep, often subtle riches in the soul of the other. Giving attention to one side usually helps the other. As you get to know the other deeply, you will discover much about yourself.

Moore's inspiring words capture the synergy between knowing ourselves and knowing the other, which is the essence of friendship flow. His words helped me emphasize how becoming aware of something in myself, such as my desires and fears, opens my eyes to these features in the other.

As I have learned to be a friend, I have often found that I must confront the differences between myself and my companion, as well as the gap between what I know and what I do not know. These differences create a tension of opposites, for which I usually try to find a balance, or closure. Moore proposes a different, helpful approach, though. His idea is to accept the tension without trying to resolve it, while continuing to act: it is the tension of opposites in which I seek to know myself and to know the other, while realizing that much of both of us will remain unknowable.

Moore helped me realize that honouring the mystery through action means living with the tension of opposites, which is both sustaining and difficult. My leap of faith in meeting this challenge is sustained by the flow of friendship underlying my efforts.

These very brief quotations are only a sample of how Moore's ideas clarify the notion that to honour friendship is to honour the mystery of the other and how friendship bridges the gap between the known and the unknown.

John O'Donohue's Ideas of "The Mystery of Friendship"

The title of John O'Donohue's book, *Anam Cara*, means "soul friend"; his ideas about the "mystery of friendship" is an inspiring integration of both the Spirit of Friendship and honouring its mystery. O'Donohue's description of the mystery of friendship emphasizes the unique human capacity to transcend the mystery: "It's strange to be here. The mystery never leaves you alone.... A world lives within you. No one else can bring you news of this inner world," and "No one else can undertake this task for you. You are the one and only threshold of this inner world." O'Donohue eloquently emphasizes the special opportunity to evoke the precious individual potential tucked away in our inner resources. His emphasis on the possibilities of our inner exploration offered me a beacon, lighting my way into the shrouded world of the mystery of the other. Like Thomas Moore, he believes that friendship bridges the gap of the unknown:

> Nowhere else is there such intimate and frightening access to the mysterium. Friendship is that sweet grace that liberates us to approach, recognize, and inhabit this adventure.

"The secret affinity within us," as O'Donohue says, is the mystical spirit that comes from beginning with ourselves. O'Donohue's central theme, *Anam Cara* or "soul friend," has also been a profound influence on my understanding of friendship. His description of a soul friend as completely accepting no matter what — distance, time, or disagreement — has been an important influence on all of my beliefs and exercises in strengthening our friendship ties.

CONVERGENCE OF IDEAS

In preparation for writing this theme, I reviewed each of these influential books, and I was delightfully surprised to find their descriptions of the essence of friendship to be so similar to one another, as well as to my views in this workshop!

MOORE:
A soulful relationship offers two difficult challenges: one, to know oneself … and two, to get to know the deep, often subtle riches in the soul of the other. Giving attention to one side usually helps the other. As you get to know the other deeply, you will discover much about yourself.

O'DONOHUE:
In the growth and homecoming is the unlooked-for bonus in the act of loving another. Love begins with paying attention to others, with an act of gracious self-forgetting. This is the condition in which we grow.

Comparing these two meaning-dense paragraphs reveals many similarities. For example, the emphasis on attention, the need for letting go of your Ego — O'Donohue's lovely phrase, "an act of gracious self-forgetting," captures it best — and most of all, the possibility of friendship to aid in our own growth, to realize our potential. All of this reminded me of one-workshop participant's observations, which I quoted earlier but is worth repeating:

Making new connections with others is how I grow and change as a person. This requires the suspension of my personal agenda in exchange for a relational one. Relationships begin and grow when both persons are present in the experience together. It is then that we can journey together.

Another important the convergence of the ideas is that being a friend to others is a surprising route to becoming what we may be. Moore's observation that "you will discover much about yourself" and O'Donohue's "unlooked-for bonus" are harbingers of my notion of becoming aware of the secret of our human potential through friendship, as well as the ideas in Ferrucci's recently published book *The Power of Kindness: The Unexpected Effects of Leading a Compassionate Life*. He echoes Ornish's *Love and Survival* with his major theme of the "survival of the kindest."

MY EXPERIENCE OF HONOURING THE MYSTERY IN MY WORK

For many years I took my work as a psychologist very seriously, believing that it called for me to understand both the enormous variation between individuals, as well as how and why they engaged in their personal ventures. I tried applying all of the principles of the scientific method, especially logical analysis, to achieve this goal, but was very frustrated at my failure. I also realized, as I turned my attention within and reflected on myself, that there was a lot that I could not understand. I began to honour the mystery out of necessity. I didn't abandon my attempt to understand the human condition, but my efforts were imbued with my respect and acceptance of the mysterious nature of our lives. I felt a great sense of relief as honouring the mystery of human nature lightened my professional burden. I also experienced the "unlooked-for bonus" of gaining a deeper understanding of the human venture.

PLANNING THE WORKSHOP

Having summarized how my past experiences have influenced the workshop, I will conclude with a description of how I planned the workshop. I will begin with finding the right theme and title, and then describe how I organized the specific workshop exercises.

Finding the Right Theme and Title

Like many people, I often took friendship for granted; consequently it was a long time before I realized that it was the right theme for my workshop. It was a slow process that began by compiling all of the exercises from my workshops into one workbook, called *Connecting with Ourselves*. I knew I wanted to write one more book to complete my Inside-Out trilogy, but none of my ideas seemed quite right. Because of my powerful personal experience as a participant in the Open Your Heart support group, I tried themes such as Open Your Heart and Living from My Heart, but they didn't click. Then I tried a specific action guide that I found important, with the title *Lighten Up to Open Up*, but this also seemed to be too limited.

With apologies to Parker Palmer and his book *The Courage to Teach*, I tried *The Courage to Trust Yourself*, but this seemed to repeat my earlier book. My final unsuccessful attempt was a draft manuscript for a short book called *Wake Up to Love*. I still like the "wake up" idea, because I continue to believe that most people need a strong wake-up call, in the form of a personal difficulty or crisis, to stop them from taking things for granted and start reflecting on their inner resources. Even though I learned a great deal writing about love and acknowledged its vital importance, it did not feel exactly right. But it did provide the foundation for the appearance of friendship in my work.

Once the idea of learning to be a friend came to light, everything seemed to fall into place. At last I found the write title: *To Be a Friend*.

ORGANIZING THE EXERCISES

I based my initial planning of this friendship workshop based on two earlier principles: first, the sequence from Self to Other to Relationship (which originated much earlier with the New Three *R*'s in 1978); and second, the principles of my earlier workshops: Letting Go, Opening Up, and Accepting. The first version of the workshop exercises were a very neat 3x3 diagram combining the three aims,

Letting go, Opening up, and Accepting, within the three areas of focus, Self, Other, and Relationship as follows:

You begin with a focus on your **SELF**:

THEME ONE	THEME TWO	THEME THREE
Letting Go of Personal Obstacles	Opening to Yourself	Accepting Yourself

Next, you focus on the **OTHER**:

THEME FOUR	THEME FIVE	THEME SIX
Letting Go of Your Ego	Opening to Others	Accepting Others

Finally, you focus on your **RELATIONSHIP**:

THEME SEVEN	THEME EIGHT	THEME NINE
Letting Go of Old, Fixed Expectations	Opening to Changes in Friends	Accepting Friendship and That's All

In the first focus, on the Self, the second theme was an exercise aimed at openning your breathing and senses. In the second focus, on the Other, Theme Six consisted of exercises geared toward learning to accept both similarities and differences in others. And in the third focus, on Relationships, Theme Eight was based on learning to accept and encourage changes both in your friend and in your relationship.

Once the "Little Professor" inside me saw this neat 3x3 diagram, he smiled with delight, believing that now that the workshop was on clear, logical footing it was almost finished. Fortunately, another part of me responded very differently: "Wait a minute, this diagram is *too* logical, too neat, there is no room for other possibilities. It's all from the head with no heart." With this insight, I began to redevelop the exercises in the workshop, informed by this neat diagram, but also taking account of how I felt and my responses while learning to be a friend. I like to imagine that my final approach to developing these sixteen workshop exercises came from both my head and my heart, but time will tell.

Letting go, Opening up, and Accepting are still the underlying foundation for the exercises and they are also the basis for the development of personal action guides, which I describe in the next section.

Part Two:

A Workshop for Learning to Be a Friend

Unlike most books on friendship, this book invites your participation in a workshop of activities to help you actively learn more about being a friend. I realize that a workshop format is an unusual way to communicate in a book, and I wish we could meet together for a weekend, face-to-face workshop. I am also aware that becoming an active participant is more demanding and time consuming than passively reading expert advice. Nevertheless, I believe strongly that active participation is necessary in learning to be a friend. My belief in active participation comes both from my professional experience offering hundreds of workshops in personal development, and my own personal experience of taking responsibility for my own learning and following my own advice.

I hope that through your engagement in the workshop activities in this book, I can communicate with you through your actions and we can learn together.

PRINCIPLES OF THE WORKSHOP

The principles of this workshop are based on my personal beliefs about friendship, which have developed through my experience in both my personal and professional life, as I have already discussed. My increasing awareness of the central importance of the Spirit of Friendship in our lives was the spark igniting my desire to offer this workshop.

The workshop is organized into three sections according to the basic features of friendship: Self, Other, and Relationship. Each section contains five exercises aimed at encouraging your acceptance of that specific feature, whether it be Accepting the Self, Accepting the Other, or Accepting Your Friendship Ties. Following the exercise on Welcoming the Spirit of Friendship, the workshop concludes with a summary exercise on Bringing Out Your Meaning of Friendship.

The key principles the workshop embodies are:

- Being a Friend Means to Be Friends with Yourself

- Being a Friend Means Accepting the Other Person
- Being a Friend Means Honouring Your Friendship Ties
- Being a Friend Means Welcoming the Spirit of Friendship
- Bring Out Your Meaning of Friendship: Your Meaning Map

The essential action of being a friend is to attentively accept the object of friendship, whether it be yourself, the other person, or your friendship ties. Acceptance is the basis of being a friend. Accepting yourself means to do so completely, accepting another means to accept the humanity of the other person regardless of your differences, and, finally, accepting friendship ties means to accept the changing nature of your relationships while supported by an underlying trust. In all cases, learning to be a friend involves giving your undivided attention to the object of friendship. Focusing your attention is the essential first step in each of the workshop exercises because it is a tangible indicator of how you honour the importance of friendship. You show the strength of your commitment to friendship by the intensity of attention in your acceptance.

1. BEING A FRIEND MEANS TO BE FRIENDS WITH YOURSELF

We usually think of friendship as a relationship between two people, but the key to friendship is becoming friends with yourself. Based on my book, *Beginning with Ourselves* (1987), my earlier workshops offered opportunities for participants to learn about their personal beliefs and inner resources. As one of the earlier workshop participants commented after the workshop:

> I really know more than I thought, and the knowledge comes from self. I have learned to become friends with myself.

When I began with myself, I was surprised at what I found. I discovered that my personal desires as well as my deepest fears, my inner capabilities, and my vulnerabilities formed a unique pattern, which made me the distinct person I am. As I attempted to accept all these parts of myself, warts and all, I became friends with myself.

My experience of becoming friends with myself brought two important insights. First, I saw that not only was my pattern of inner parts unique, but that this was true for others: each of us is distinctly different in some ways. Second, although we are different in the specific pattern of our beliefs, we are all alike in that each one of us possesses desires and fears, capabilities and vulnerabilities that guide our lives. As I thought about my being like every other person in some ways, it helped me understand what it means to be human. Our common human qualities no longer seemed a remote abstraction, but a concrete reality as I understood that no matter how different our beliefs, each one of us is alike in being guided by our personal desires and fears.

2. BEING A FRIEND MEANS ACCEPTING THE OTHER PERSON

Accepting the Other's Humanity

When I offer my friendship to another person, whether they are a stranger, acquaintance, close friend, or family member, my first priority is to accept the person as a human being like myself, guided by the same desires and fears. In the case of someone who is like me and agrees with me, it is easy to appreciate their humanity. However, it is much more difficult to genuinely accept another person who is very different from myself, especially when we disagree strongly in our beliefs.

I cannot be a friend to everybody, but I would like to be able to offer my friendship even to people with whom I disagree, if it seems worthwhile. Even though it might be challenging to converse with someone with strongly different views on moral or political matters, I have been able to do so by following two guidelines. First, I make sure that my own beliefs are safely set aside so that I can take in the other's different beliefs free of any threat they may pose to my beliefs. Second, I tell myself that I can accept someone without necessarily agreeing with them. Acceptance is different from agreement. My motive for accepting someone with whom I disagree is to better understand them, as well as to clarify my own beliefs through our conversation. Unfortunately, despite its value, it hasn't always been easy for me to accept others with whom I disagree. However, in those rare instances where I have maintained the courage to do so, I have always been rewarded by learning more about them, and about myself.

I have found a very helpful action guide for offering friendship, whether to a person who is different or like me. I "Accept ... That's All." In the case of those with whom I disagree, "that's all" means "I do not need to agree with them. I accept them ... that's all." For those who are like me, "that's all" means "I have no ulterior motives such as, what's in it for me. I accept them ... that's all." In sum, I try to accept the other's humanity and accept the person with neither expectations of personal gain or concerns about their disagreement. I want to be a friend ... that's all.

In accepting another I try to offer my complete attention because I know how rewarding it is to receive undivided attention from a friend. When someone gives you their complete attention, it creates the feeling of being a worthy person, which will buoys you confidence. This is followed by an even stronger feeling of complete connected to the friend, of being truly in touch. During my earlier incarnation as a psychotherapist, I realized the essential importance of giving my complete attention to the client. It is not only clients in psychotherapy who yearn to be completely listened to; I believe that most people would gladly pay for an hour in which they were carefully listened to and completely accepted.

Making Space for the Other

To attentively accept a person, I need to make space within myself to take them in. Put simply, if I am full of myself and my own concerns, there is no room for the other. It is as if I am about to host a party and my home is so full of my own possessions that there's no room for the guests. I need to clear things away to make space so that my guests will feel welcome and comfortable.

The first principle, being a friend to myself, allowed me to become aware of my personal beliefs, so now it is time to set these safely aside: this is the transition from *me* to *we*, or as one of the workshop participants expressed it clearly:

> Making new connections with others is how I grow and change as a person. This requires the suspension of my personal agenda in exchange for a relational one. Relationships begin and grow when both persons are present in the experience together. It is then that we can journey together.

Becoming a welcoming host and shifting from *me* to *we* are helpful images, but in some ways my best guide is a simple action statement: Let my ego go. My ego contains all of my personal desires and self-aggrandizing wishes, which are a part of me, but when it comes to being a friend, they need to be "suspended." This phrase — let my ego go — crystallized in my mind when I imagined hearing Paul Robeson's deep voice singing the well-know song, "Let… my… people… go." It became a musical mantra for my inner song, "Let… my… ego… go."

3. BEING A FRIEND MEANS HONOURING YOUR FRIENDSHIP TIES

When considering how to sustain and strengthen my relationships with family members and close friends, I began noting that our friendships had developed through many interactions in which we each formed expectations of one another. These interlocking expectations may be as simple as who usually speaks first, or they may involve sharing responsibility for mutual projects. Each of our expectations is a tiny thread and these threads gradually combine to form a tapestry of trust that binds our friendship. This is our friendship tie. While our expectations are expressed in words, the underlying bond of trust is beyond words, it is the deep and abiding essence of our being friends.

Accepting Change

The bond of trust to a family member or close friend is gradually formed through our interlocking expectations, but once in place, the bond no longer depends on specific expectations: it has a life of its own.

This dilemma presents itself when my friend changes in some way that no longer meets my expectations. In such cases, I must realize that when you change, our relationship also changes, and it is up to me to change my expectations accordingly. In order for our relationship to continue to flourish, I need to be willing to change; the underlying trust in the relationship does not change but may become even stronger.

This principle of willingness to change was elucidated by the lyrics of love songs of the 30s, which often emphasized men requesting that women never change — "Don't change a hair for me, not if you care for me" — but, of course, we all change. I find living by this principle is one of the most challenging of my beliefs, because it requires risking the basis of our relationship when we shift our interlocking expectations. What helps me change is my realization that my doing so will allow both of us to grow and develop.

Focusing on Your Friendship Ties

When I focus on being a friend to a family member or someone close to me, I shift my attention to the trust we have developed over the course of our relationship. This means I need to carefully consider how my actions influence our friendship. In order to give priority to nurturing our relationship,

I try to consider this question before I act: will my actions help or hinder our relationship? Of course, I don't consider this question in all of my actions and, even when I do, I am not always able to follow its guidance. But simply keeping it in mind helps me remember the importance of our relationship so that I don't take it for granted.

We must also take another look at the old adage: honesty is the best policy. I may want to tell my friend something out of a desire to be honest, but, on further consideration may realize that it might actually be detrimental to the relationship to express my honest feelings. It is a delicate balance that needs to be considered within the context of the specific circumstances.

4. BEING A FRIEND MEANS WELCOMING THE SPIRIT OF FRIENDSHIP

Perhaps the most important lesson I've learned from trying to live my beliefs was discovering the Spirit of Friendship, and its essential role in my life.

By applying our beliefs to our daily lives, we can often be opened to new insights. For instance, my actions may encourage friendship in my life, but I cannot control its flow: the flow of friendship comes from the Spirit of Friendship. Nothing has had more of a profound impact on my learning to be a friend than my awakening to this magical and mystical Spirit, which determines how my friends and I will experience our interactions.

Welcoming the Spirit of Friendship means that, in all my actions aimed at being a friend, I act from my heart. It means I place my trust in the Spirit of Friendship as I accept my friend. Accepting the Spirit relieves the heavy burden of trying to control what happens: I want to take responsibility for myself and maximize the possibility of friendship flourishing in my life. On the other hand, I am relieved that the outcome depends on the Spirit of Friendship. I learned to honour and trust the Spirit of Friendship gradually, by working through each of the workshop exercises and I believe this will be true for you as well. Becoming aware of the Spirit of Friendship is an indescribable experience involving the warm and gentle flow of affection.

5. BRING OUT YOUR MEANING OF FRIENDSHIP: YOUR MEANING MAP

This final exercise offers you an opportunity to summarize your personal meaning of friendship by creating a friendship "meaning map." To do so, focus on the various ways you experience friendship: how you perceive it through its sound, sight, touch, and other senses; how you feel when you experience friendship; how you express friendship through your actions; and how you express it in your thoughts through words. By creating your own meaning map, you make friendship your own. When you become aware of your personal meaning and express it in your own terms, you can apply your awareness to your actions to try to live your beliefs.

WHAT YOU WILL GIVE TO THE WORKSHOP

Up until now, I have made general suggestions about learning to be a friend, such as "to have a friend, you need to be a friend" and "open your heart to the Spirit of Friendship," in order to encourage you to think more actively about friendship. The workshop exercises offer specific, personal activities to help you meet these general aims.

When you make the decision to learn to be a friend, engaging in the workshop exercises is the specific means of your acting on your choice. Each workshop exercise is based on the Three *A*'s: Attention, Awareness, and Action. Specifically, you are asked to:

Focus attention	Pay special attention to the topic of the exercise, e.g. your breathing
Be aware	Express your awareness in a short action guide, e.g. stop judging
Take action	Apply your action guide to your life, e.g. make space to listen to your companion

FOCUS ATTENTION

What you pay attention to has an enormous influence on how you live your life. Take a moment to observe your own focus of attention at the moment. You are partially focused on this printed page, but are you distracted by other things? Imagine that your attention is a flashlight with an adjustable beam: you can choose to focus the beam wherever you wish and you can adjust its intensity. So it is with your attention; you can focus it where you want and you can control its intensity.

Many people don't pay attention to their inner beliefs because they have gotten into the habit of focusing solely on the outside world. The most compelling reasons for their riveted attention to the outside world are the numbers that have become the most prevalent influences in our lives: 24/7. The unrelenting external pressure of 24/7 is a magnetic force that many are unable to resist. Our eyes and ears are also constantly bombarded by advertisements through TV, Internet, radio, and print; even outside the city we are surrounded by sight and sound pollution.

Not only have the external influences on our attention increased, but the value of undivided attention has been undermined by the cultural pressure to multi-task, which divides our attention. Because of this increasing pressure, people believe it is more important to do several things at once, at the risk of performing poorly, than to focus on completing a single action well. The clearest example, of course, is driving while talking on a cellphone, which leads to an increase in the number of accidents. Because of all this multi-tasking, we find it much more difficult to offer the essential ingredient of being a friend: our complete and undivided attention.

This workshop offers opportunities for you to learn how to control your focus; both what you focus on and the intensity of your focus. As the workshop proceeds, you will pay attention to different aspects of friendship. You begin with a focus on yourself, then shift your attention to the other person, and finally focus on your friendship ties. Learning to shift from Self to Other to Friendship Ties will help you learn to become aware of and to control your focus of attention. Like changing any long-standing habit, it is not easy to change your focus of attention, but with patience and practise you will be able to regain control of your attention.

BE AWARE

Your capacity to be aware of your experience is one of your most valuable personal possessions. Just like attention, you can control your awareness of either the outer experience or your inner life. Awareness is not an exotic abstraction; it is the most basic experience of being alive. Personal awareness is how you are right now as you read this; that is, what is in your mind at this present moment. To be aware and completely present is an important part of being a friend.

The workshops emphasize inner awareness: learning more about your own beliefs, as well as your hidden resources. Imagine you are exploring your inner territory to discover your beliefs and hidden resources. As an inner explorer, you map the territory by naming your newfound beliefs in your own private language.

Gaining awareness of your beliefs is the essential first step in living your beliefs. You might discover, as I have, that humour is very important in your being with others. But to take action on a belief, it must be expressed in a short, clear action guide that you can follow. Even though you might easily write a paragraph or more describing why humour is important, you cannot carry such a long description in your head. You might compress the complexity of your belief in humour with an action guide such as "Lighten Up" or "Look for the Foolishness." In any case, try to express it in your own private language so that you can complete the final step of taking action to live your belief.

TAKE ACTION

No matter how inspiring your awareness is, it will gradually fade away unless you put it into action. You may consider how to express your friendship to another and decide on various courses of action. The important thing is that you do take action. Just do it, as the slogan says.

As I emphasized earlier, the success of taking action depends on how clearly you express your awareness in an action guide. You might believe that friendship is more likely to flourish if you temporarily suspend your critical judgment, for instance, which you could compress into a summary, such as "Stop Judging." In my own case, I needed an action guide for my belief in unconditional acceptance, a belief that was too complex and abstract for practical use. My belief was strong, but describing it required several paragraphs. Therefore, to apply it, I came to use the guide: "Accept ... that's all."

Taking action is not only valuable for consolidating your beliefs, but it may also lead to new insights. I learned that when I try to lighten up, while it doesn't eliminate personal obstacles that may have blocked my ability to open up to a friendship, the obstacle diminishes in size so that I am better able to deal with it. Actions not only speak louder than words, but they often reveal new understandings both in and beyond words.

WHAT YOU WILL RECEIVE FROM THE WORKSHOP

Participating in these exercises is an incredible indication of your commitment to friendship, and you will also receive many benefits.

When you are in touch with the Spirit of Friendship, even your health and well-being improve. Workshop participation does not guarantee the immediate flow of friendship, but you will feel your own capability to initiate the flow as you become a better friend. Each of us will experience this gradual welcoming of friendship in our own unique way. You may feel a sense of warmth, a feeling of completeness, or you may simply smile; but whatever your reaction, you will realize that the Spirit of Friendship is always within you.

The workshop exercises are aimed at encouraging the Spirit of Friendship in your life, and you will likely experience its warm and magical flow. Whatever its immediate effect, the choice to be a friend carries its own rewards. The acceptance of the other person and our friendship ties is a confidence booster, whatever the result.

It is understandable that in your initial attempts to be a friend, you will want to experience friendship in return from the other person, along with an immediate flow of friendship. However, as you gradually realize that you cannot completely control this flow, you will feel the strength that comes from your choice to offer friendship, regardless of the outcome.

Like everything worthwhile in life, learning *to be* a friend takes time and patience. However, there is an added benefit in store if you stay the course. I have found that, although it initially requires considerable effort to pay attention, be aware, and take action, it became a comfortable habit over time. Perhaps eventually my learning to be a friend will become such an automatic habit that I will need to begin to pay attention again; but I will face that problem when it occurs. Here is a comment on the benefits of the workshop from an earlier participant:

The process of discovering my own potential is exciting, energizing, surprising, freeing, and sometimes difficult.

WELCOME TO THE WORKSHOP

It is time to actively start the workshop. You can participate in one of several different ways. The first possibility would be to find someone to act as a workshop leader and use the text as the basis of a face-to-face group workshop, which might take place on a weekend or over several shorter sessions. I realize this is unlikely, but it is a possibility. The second option is to locate a learning partner and engage in the exercises together at convenient times. The final option is to participate on your own. To engage in the exercises on your own is the most challenging option, but it can also be very rewarding. Doing the workshop on your own calls for a strong desire for success, but will also bring with it some surprising benefits.

The workshop contains fifteen exercises to help you learn to be a friend. Each exercise offers an opportunity to bring out your specific belief so that you can apply it in your life. You need to record your belief in your own words so that you will have a specific action guide to follow. Recording your beliefs is not only essential for taking action, but it also acknowledges the importance of your new insights, making them accessible for future reference.

The workshop exercises are organized into three primary sections with a final concluding activity:

I.   To Be a Friend with Yourself
II. To Be a Friend with Others
III. To Strengthen Your Friendship Ties
IV. Concluding Exercise: Bringing Out Your Meaning of Friendship

I. To Be a Friend with Yourself

Learning to be a friend begins by turning your attention to yourself, or as an earlier workshop participant put it, by becoming friends with yourself:

> I really know more than I thought, and the knowledge comes from Self. I have learned to become friends with myself.

Beginning with yourself lays the foundation for friendship in several ways. First, learning to be present to yourself helps you to be present and attentive to others. Second, when you accept all of yourself — your strengths and your foibles — you will feel more worthy of being a friend to others. Third, your self-acceptance will put you in touch with your own sense of being human, which in turn reminds you that others, too, are human. Fourth, bringing your beliefs out in the open offers another, less obvious benefit: it enables you to set them safely aside when you accept another person with very different beliefs. You can temporarily take the other person in without any threat to your beliefs.

The key to these exercises is to appreciate all parts of yourself. We often fail to appreciate our breathing and our senses. To appreciate them means you must stop taking yourself for granted and give it the attention it deserves. Putting the spotlight on these aspects of yourself is a little like the Fan Appreciation Day sports teams hold. Why not hold a Self-Appreciation Day? Remember: to appreciate is to accept whole-heartedly, and this is the basis of all friendship.

Each exercise is based on the Three *A*'s: Attention, Awareness, and Action. In the first exercise on your breathing, you begin by focusing attention on your breathing by noticing that you are taking air in and out: to become aware of your own breathing. Finally, you apply your awareness to your daily actions by taking time out during the day to appreciate your breathing. Here are the five exercises in this section:

1. Appreciating Your Breathing
2. Opening Your Senses
3. Accepting Your Capabilities
4. Accepting Your Foolishness
5. Letting Go of Obstacles

EXERCISE 1:
APPRECIATING YOUR BREATHING

Like the beating of our hearts, we take our breathing for granted. Fortunately, we don't have to consciously control our breathing and we often only recognize it when we're having difficulty breathing. This exercise offers such an opportunity to appreciate and to become friends with your breathing.

Attention

Stop reading for a moment and turn your complete attention to your breath. Try to focus your attention on the air itself and its movement, as it comes in through your nose, enters your lungs, and returns through your mouth.

Awareness

Allow your attention to sprout antennae of curiosity and become aware of the specific features of your breathing: what is it like right now in your body? Begin by carefully following a single intake of air as it enters your nostrils, moves down your throat forcing your chest to expand, and then reverses its course. How does your body feel as you inhale and exhale? Where do you sense it most clearly? In your nostrils as it comes in and out, in your throat, or in your chest? As you continue following your breathing, do you notice any improvement, any slight change in your body with your regular breathing?

Spend a little time varying the pace and depth of your breathing. First, breathe quickly and rapidly for a few moments to get a feeling of what this is like. Next, breathe slowly and deeply for a time to become aware of what this is like. Finally, spend a few more moments with your eyes closed, breathing normally, to appreciate it in any way you choose. How do you feel when you have nothing to do but breathe?

Take a few moments to jot down a summary of appreciation on the topic, "What I discovered about my breathing." This brief summary of your awareness will serve to guide you as you appreciate your breath in your actions.

Action

Apply what you have learned about your breathing to your daily life by stopping for a few moments, two or three times a day, over the next few days to focus on your breath. Take a "time out" of two or three minutes and repeat what you did in the exercise by closing your eyes and breathing more deeply. Breathing is very personal and you may develop your own way of honouring your breathing. Become friends with your breathing: you won't find a more valuable friend. Summarize your experience in a short paragraph, "How I have learned to appreciate and apply my breathing."

This exercise is based on the belief that controlling your breathing is one of your unique personal possessions. That is why it focused on your discovering what your own breathing is like and accepting its personal value. While other approaches to breath control, such as yoga, may be very valuable, the first step is to become aware of and appreciate your own unique pattern of breathing. You will be surprised at how much you learn by attending to your breathing. Just as you flourish when your friend gives you complete attention, your breathing will flourish when you offer it your complete attention.

How This Exercise Worked For Me

From my yoga teacher I learned a wonderful expression, "All you have to do is breathe." This statement reminds me not only of breathing's significance, but also of the relief I get from focusing on my breathing. I am simply being alive and the effortlessness of this reminder is anything but basic in its enormous value. All of my other concerns and issues temporarily fade away as I am aware of the precious gift of my being alive.

My personal instructions consist of directing myself to breathe, to relax, and to clear my mind. I begin by focusing on my breath as it comes in and goes out, giving all my attention to this movement of air in my body. After a moment, I shift my attention slightly to identify any tension or discomfort I may be experiencing and then I allow my exhalation:

I let go of this tension. Breathing out is letting go of tension. Finally, after anoher moment, I shift my thoughts once more to identify any remaining concerns I have and I breathe them away, to be reclaimed later. Breathing out is a way of letting go of mind clutter. I sometimes stop during the day when I feel out of kilter and go through these breathing exercises to restore my balance

EXERCISE 2:
OPENING YOUR SENSES

You can read this sentence because you can see, yet you likely take your sense of sight for granted. The same is true for your ability to hear, touch, smell, and taste. Like our breathing, we appreciate the vitality of our senses only through the shock of experiencing difficulty. I know this through first-hand experience: I lost most of my central vision a few years ago. My personal shock of recognition awakened my awareness of the increased importance of my other senses to compensate for the loss.

You don't have to wait for sensory catastrophe to realize the precious gift of your senses, and this exercise is designed to help you appreciate and open them all the time.

The attentive acceptance of your senses is not only important for becoming a friend to yourself, but it also lays the foundation for becoming friends with others: your senses provide the connecting channels through which you attend to the other person. The more open your senses, the more you are in touch with the moment; the more you are present, and the more you are able to attentively accept the other person, the more you open your senses, the more you open your heart.

Attentive acceptance calls for all your senses, but you will find that some of your senses are more open than others. Many find their visual channel most dominant, others find the aural to be their strongest channel. In any case, as you note the differential openness of your channels, accept this distinctive pattern as your personal signature. It is also true that you can choose to develop your less dominant channels, but that is not the present purpose.

Attention

Look around the room and select an object that catches your attention, perhaps a plant or a painting. When you have made your selection, imagine that you have never experienced this object before and try to take it in as completely as possible. Attend to each of your five senses in turn. First focusing your eyes on the object, then listening carefully for any sound. If there is no sound, imagine what sound it might make or the sounds you might associate with it. Next, touch the object and, finally, consider how it might smell and taste in your imagination.

Awareness

As you focus attention on each sense, spend some time allowing your impression to float through your mind so that you can capture them thoroughly. Allow yourself to free-associate with the meaning this object evokes for you. When you focus on sound, imagine that it has a voice and can speak and sing. What would it sound like? As you are taking the object in, ask yourself whether it reminds you of any other objects or experiences. In opening your senses to this object, try to understand it as completely as possible so that you could describe it to another person or write about it. Use your sensory intake to create meaning out of this object. Feel free to make notes as you make new meanings.

When you have finished taking in and reviewing the object, come back and look at it again. Has opening up to it made a difference? Before this exercise you probably took the object for granted, but now it has more meaning, more value to you. Take a moment to consider how you might apply this kind of opening up to other parts of your life, to enhance their meaning. As you will see in later exercises on being a friend to others, opening your senses is a vital means of connecting.

Action

Try to apply what you learned about opening your senses to something in your life that you want to understand more fully; it might be another person on an object. Sometime during the next day, stop and focus your attention on an item of your choosing for a few moments to become aware of its unique qualities. Notice the effects of your openness. Often, this will produce both surprising new insights into whatever you opened to, and a sense of confidence in having discovered a new approach to enhancing your understanding of your experience.

HOW THIS EXERCISE WORKED FOR PARTICIPANTS

This exercise allowed me to consider the importance of taking time for my own mental processes — to consider my own personal qualities, knowledge, and experience, which I have acquired throughout my life journey. It allowed me to "put it all together" and give these processes visual representation. I am a visual person so this has been very helpful to me. It made me respect that there is time to sit back and get refocused.

Sometimes there are unexpected, surprising reflections, such as these from former participants:

> When reflecting on my openness to sensory channels, I realize that different sensory channels are open to different degrees. Furthermore, some sensory channels are connected more closely to the mind, some access my feelings, and some connect more closely to the inner body. This is important information for me as I can try to access or develop certain channels to access different areas of myself.

> I am a very analytical person and dominated by my mind. My inner critic is also very analytical and resides in the mind. My visual channel is very strong and leads me to my mind and analytical side. The connection is very strong between seeing and thinking. It is difficult for visual stimuli to connect to my feelings. Often in order to feel something I will need to close my eyes. Hearing is a sensory channel that connects me with both my mind and my feelings. Feelings can be tapped into through music and hearing the sounds of nature. Music can be particularly powerful in terms of soothing my feelings and my soul. Again, to help me listen, sometimes I will close my eyes so I can really hear what is going on.

Although smell is not a dominant sensory channel, smell has a strong connection to my feelings and my body. It often bypasses the mind and triggers feelings and bodily sensations that may be either positive or negative.

Touch is a sensory channel that is very under-developed and limited. Perhaps because of past traumatic experiences touch sensation usually goes to the mind and often through the offices of my inner critic before I can experience touch. I have difficulty "letting go to experience touch in my feelings or my inner body." While through this course I have realized that my inner critic mobilizes my mind to act as an intermediary to "vet" my touch experiences and make sure they are okay.

Taste is a sensory channel that evokes feelings very strongly and directly. Under emotional stress I may eat to calm and soothe myself. The tastes of different foods evoke strong feelings and inner body sensations.

These reflections illustrate several important features of exploring our channels. First, the personal insights came from the participant's genuine curiosity and willingness to be surprised about his inner life. Second, there is an awareness that the various channels need to be considered in relation to one another. Finally, these insights are presented for their personal value, with no implication that the ideas would apply to everyone. Some of these ideas about the relation between sensory channels and other channels may ring true for you as well, but the main purpose is to pique your curiosity about how these channels are related for you.

EXERCISE 3:
ACCEPTING YOUR CAPABILITIES

Accepting a friend begins by focusing your attention on your friend's best features; this is especially true for becoming friends with yourself. This exercise invites you to recall experiences of yourself at your best, in order to accept your positive features. Recalling yourself when you were at your best allows you to consider why you were doing well, so you can identify your underlying beliefs. Once revealed, your beliefs can guide your daily actions, which will increase the likelihood of further positive experiences. Taking time to appreciate yourself at your best often reveals an unexpected ally, a hidden resource, a new friend. It is as if you have taken yourself so much for granted that you failed to realize your capabilities.

Of course, self-acceptance involves accepting your vulnerabilities as well as your strengths, but we will get to those in the next exercise. For now, let's focus on yourself at your best.

Attention

Take a few moments to focus your attention on your past experience, and emphasize positive experiences, times when you were doing well, performing at your best. These may be situations at work or at home. Select one of these positive experiences that you can recall clearly in order to focus on it in this exercise.

Awareness

Now that you have identified your positive experience, follow these steps to become aware of your actions and why they occurred.

1. Take a few moments to recall this positive situation in as much detail as possible. Close your eyes and remember what it was like: how you felt at the time, what was said, and as many details as you can about what happened. Try to be in the experience, not simply observe it. Be there.

2. Open your eyes and jot down the highlights of the positive situation. Don't be concerned about the

order; just list the main features you remembered about this experience.

3. Holding these highlights in mind, try to describe why you think it worked so well. Describe the reasons for your success: how do you understand or make sense of this situation? What did you do to help bring about this positive experience?

4. Consider why you believe this happened and translate your analysis into action language. Try to summarize your understanding into a short action guide, which you can follow to try to create another positive experience. It is for your use, so express the action guide in your own words.

Participants who completed this exercise brought out a wide variety of inner beliefs. Among them were "Trust Myself," "Be Patient," "Work Harder," "Take it Easy," "Be Quiet and Listen," "Stop Judging," "Let Them Know What I Know," and "Keep Smiling." When you read another person's action guide, it often seems simple, obvious, and even trite. However, as you will discover when you develop your own action guides, they have significant personal meaning when they are based on your beliefs. These phrases compress the complexity of your beliefs into short action guides that you can follow as you live your belief.

Action

Make sure you have a clear statement of your action guide, perhaps jotting it on a card. Keep it in your mind for the next day and try to apply it whenever it seems appropriate. As you apply it, you may need to clarify it further. Be patient in identifying and applying your own action guides, remembering that what is most important is that the belief and action guide have meaning for you.

Applying your own beliefs builds your confidence in a way that nothing else can. It is tangible evidence that you know something, and, equally important, that you have found a friend. As one participant put it: "I now believe that I can deal with my difficult problems by using what is inside of me ... my own strength."

HOW THIS EXERCISE WORKED FOR A PARTICIPANT

Following is an example of what another participant learned from this exercise by recalling a rather unusual experience:

Positive Experience: I am sitting with my father-in-law at the bedside of my mother-in-law, on the evening of her death. Listening to the story of their life together and the journey they were on.

Highlights I remember are the qualities of respect and openness, the feeling of serenity and peacefulness. The air was filled with a faith and an optimism that seemed juxtaposed to the impending death of our loved one. I remember the sense of sacredness about the words that he was saying, as they held some personal wisdom for me. The sound of silence, which usually frightens me, made me feel peaceful.

The softness of her hand in mine and the gentle feeling of her skin against mine was full of life. I remember feeling light, energized and serene all at once. I was not conscious of my body, only of the letting go and opening up as I listened, heard and felt the moment. The solitude of the moment and my connection to them are etched in my memory.

Why? This happened because I let go and allowed myself to experience the moment. I did not feel compelled to offer comfort, wisdom, or advice. I was simply there listening and open to what the moment offered. I was not afraid of the experience.

Action: What is striking about this for me is the idea of being in the moment, freezing time, being still enough to enjoy the simplicity of the time. It offered the action guide "JUST BE" and I found following this suggestion to be very valuable.

This account shows how bringing out your underlying belief in a very brief action guide can have great practical and personal value. Try to apply your own guide in the same way.

EXERCISE 4:
ACCEPTING YOUR FOOLISHNESS

Because being a friend means accepting all of the person, shortcomings as well as talents, this exercise focuses on appreciating and taking in your own less-than-positive parts. The key to accepting these is to take a light-hearted view, to see the humour in your foibles. That is why the exercise emphasizes accepting your foolishness.

It is not as easy to accept your foolishness as it is to accept your strengths, so you may wonder if it is worth the trouble. But, as I have emphasized, to truly become friends with yourself, you need to accept *all* parts of yourself, including your foolish foibles. Meeting this challenge may put you in touch with yourself in a special way as you learn to laugh at yourself. When you become aware of your shortcomings, you will bring out your own humanity, which in turn sets the foundation for accepting the humanity in others: the humanity so evident in your imperfections is not only true for you, but for others as well.

This exercise is based on one experience and therefore provides only one sample of your less-positive features. You are not expected to create a catalogue and checklist of all your shortcomings. As you open to your vulnerabilities, it is important that to be gentle with yourself and not become overwhelmed by your less-than-positive features. Make sure that this exercise does not become an invitation for your inner critic to take over and exaggerate your limitations. Be gentle and light of heart.

Attention

Take a few moments to review your recent experiences, with emphasis on those times when you were less than perfect, when you did something wrong or foolish. These may be occasions when you wish you had acted differently toward another person, situations at work when you might have done better, or occasions when you were alone and did something silly. In your initial consideration of your shortcomings, you may want to select a rather small imperfection.

Awareness

Now that you have identified the specific situation, follow these steps to become aware of your actions and why they occurred.

---

1. Take a few moments to recall the situation in as much detail as possible. Close your eyes and remember what it was like: how you felt at the time, what was said, and as many details as you can about what happened.

2. Now imagine you are another person, someone who is quite open-minded and good-hearted, observing this situation. Take in what happened and accept it in a lighthearted way.

3. Next, allow yourself to converse with this observer to find out more about their view of the situation. Talk about what happened so that you can start to see your shortcoming as something human. Accept responsibility for whatever you did, but also see its foolish side.

4. Consider your choice of action first by focusing on how you feel about your imperfection — whether you can see its foolishness, or not — and second, focus on whether you want to change anything so that it will not happen again.

Action

During the next day or so, pay special attention to times when you are having difficulty and see whether there is any humour in the situation. Still remaining gentle with yourself, try to focus your attention on your own foolishness and, in so doing, the foolishness of others. It is all part of being human.

Accepting your own imperfections is a challenging task to carry out on your own, but if you proceed gradually and gently, the results can be more than worthwhile.

HOW THIS EXERCISE WORKED FOR ME

It probably tells something about my difficulty in accepting my own foolishness that I developed this exercise only recently and have not used it in earlier workshops. What I can report from my own experience is the difficulty of becoming aware of my foolishness, as well as my realization that I probably remain unaware of most of my imperfections. However, I can cite one general example.

I have had the good fortune and time to bring out short action guides for living my own personal beliefs, which I will describe in the final section. Even though I have spent much time describing these guides and realizing their value, I often fail to follow them. So when I get into trouble or experience difficulty of some kind, I almost always realize later, sometimes much later, that the difficulty occurred because of my foolishness at not following my own advice. I think of myself being especially foolish because I *know* what is best and have not followed it.

Finally, I think it would be helpful to ask a trusted family member or friend to let me know about my foolish things. This would take a lot of trust, but I may try it.

EXERCISE 5:
LETTING GO OF OBSTACLES

As you tried to appreciate and accept parts of yourself in the previous exercises, you may have encountered some obstacles. For example, if you tend to focus attention only on outside events, it can create obstacles to focusing attention within yourself. Or, if you are in the habit of always trying to control the situation and yourself, this might block your ability to appreciate some of your actions as foolish, which calls for letting go of control.

The initial purpose of developing habits is to make certain behaviours automatic, so that you don't have to make a conscious choice about every action you take. In the process of going on automatic pilot, habits may become brittle and you can fall into a rut. We need to become aware of our habits since they may block attempts to try new ways of being. We need to learn to let go, even if only temporarily, of those habits that have become obstacles.

Obstructive habits can be habitual ways of thinking that have become automatic and outside of awareness. One common obstacle is a preoccupation with the past. Another cases, is a fixation on the future and your worries about what may happen.

Whatever the preoccupation these habits literally occupy all of your mental space so that there is no room for learning to be a friend. You need to deal with this blockage by letting go of the "pre" in preoccupation. This exercise is designed to help you become aware of what it is you need to let go of, so that you can try to deal with the obstacles.

Attention

Focus your attention on the following poem, the author of which is unknown. I always read it with a focus on the question, "Does this one apply to me especially?" As you slowly read through each couplet, think about its application to you and your life.

LETTING GO does not mean to stop caring ... it means not to take responsibility for someone else.

LETTING GO is not to cut myself

---

off from others ... it's realizing I can't control others.

LETTING GO is not to try to change or blame others ... but to make the most of myself.

LETTING GO is not to care for ... but to care about.

LETTING GO is not to fix ... but to be supportive.

LETTING GO is not to be in the middle arranging ... but to be on the sidelines, cheering.

LETTING GO is not to be protective ... it's to permit another to face reality.

LETTING GO is not to deny ... but to accept.

LETTING GO is not to nag, scold or argue ... it is to search out my own shortcomings and correct them.

LETTING GO is not to adjust everything to my desires ... but to take each day as it comes, and cherish myself in it.

LETTING GO is not to criticize and regulate others ... but to be what I can become.

LETTING GO is not to regret the past ... but to grow and live for the future.

LETTING GO is to fear less and love more.

Awareness

Look back over the lines and select a few that seem significant to you. Consider them one by one, jotting down why each is important to you and how you might use it in your life.

Select one that seems especially important to you and review why it is seems so relevant. Take a moment to express it in your own terms so that you can try to actively apply it in your daily life. Jot it down on a card so you will have a reminder.

Action

For the next few days, try to follow the action guide you have selected. By trying to let go, you are changing old, ingrained habits, so be patient but persistent and keep notes on your experience.

What follows are two examples of how earlier participants used the exercise. Notice especially how they
translated the suggestion into their own terms:

> As I was reading "Letting Go," many parts of
> it touched me greatly. It was as if it was writ-
> ten especially for me. I began to realize that I
> had been stuck in negative thought patterns
> and that it was time to "let go" of these. It
> was time to change the way I handled cer-
> tain situations in my life. The one stanza that
> touched me the most was: *To let go is not to
> adjust everything to my desires but to take each
> day as it comes, and cherish myself in it.* This
> was meaningful for me because I always like
> to be in control of every situation. I don't
> like it when I feel that I am losing control.
> Therefore, I like to manipulate situations
> so that I feel comfortable. Unfortunately, I
> don't let things just occur. Sometimes I feel
> it is important to be proactive, however it is
> not always necessary to adjust situations for
> my benefit. By letting situations unfold and
> things happen I open myself up for oppor-
> tunities to surprise myself. I also give others
> the freedom to show their true selves. By
> allowing situations to naturally unfold I gain
> a better understanding of others and myself.
> By understanding myself better I can begin

to trust and cherish myself. The only way I can truly like and appreciate who I am is by understanding and trusting myself.

The second stanza that I identified with was: *To let go is not to criticize and regulate anybody but to try to become what I dream I can be.* This stanza also touched me greatly because of some of the same reasons as I mentioned above. Another reason for it having a great impact on me is the fact that I often see others' faults quickly and easily. I don't always see my faults as clearly. This statement reminded me to refrain from judging others but yet to work on becoming the best person that I can be. In other words, focus my energy positively on myself, not negatively on others.

These powerful reflections exemplify many features of letting go: the importance of beginning with ourselves, the necessity of accepting our own vulnerabilities and inadequacies, and the value of maintaining a positive and curious attitude toward the possibility of change.

In this next example, there is a need to let go of control in relation to both children and parents:

The stanza that speaks to me is the one which states: *To let go is not to fix but to be supportive.* I chose these lines because they most clearly represent my daily struggles. Here are a few of the phrases that I have heard myself say: "Don't worry; I'll help you."... "You're too young to _____. I'll do it for you"... "That's too difficult for you." (So, of course, I did it to help.) These phrases are all messages that say that I will "fix it." Without thinking it through, I send my son and my daughter a message denying them the opportunity to try. They lose the opportunity to succeed or fail on their own. I want to protect, to keep safe, and to tenderly nurture my children. I want to keep them safe from failure and disappointment. In doing so, however, I realize that I am denying them an important growth opportunity. I am denying them the opportunity to overcome failure.

Almost automatically, I reinforce my position as caregiver, competent adult, and the person in charge. Without meaning to, I force my child to choose between defiance and submission, which means that my child is receiving a reward for obedience. I make it difficult for my child to undertake self-directed activities that lead to accomplishments in unfamiliar territory. My approach is oriented toward keeping my child a child rather than encouraging personal development.

I can see that when I help by "fixing," I attempt to maintain power and control. I am ultimately trying to keep my child a child, someone that will not challenge me too much or make me feel unnecessary. I do it all in the guise of helping, but I know that sometimes I am just too impatient or unwilling to be a true teacher to my children. I know that when my children intuitively recognize what is happening, they will be resentful. This resentment may lead them to both despise me and try to manipulate me. I may be creating a child full of guile, artifice, and pretence.

After thinking about the way I treat my children, I stop to think about the way I treat my ageing parents. I hear myself saying the following things: "Oh Dad, let me read that for you" ... "Mom, that is too heavy for you; let me lift it" ... "Dad, you look so tired. Why don't you go and lie down and I will have someone finish cutting the grass." "Mother, you are confused. That isn't the way it happened." This is just a small sample but it clearly reveals my attitude. Just as I asserted myself with my children, so too have I asserted myself with my ageing parents. I realize that it is much easier to play the role of fixer, competent adult, the good daughter rather than let my parents struggle a little bit on their own. I know that when I do this, I express doubt in their abilities. If they believe me, then they will start to doubt themselves. Often they challenge me, and then they express their irritation in scolding words that often lead us to argue. My inner critic tells me to question my motives.

Notice that a key step in this participant's new awareness is the reviewing of self-talk. This is a beautiful example of how the awareness of our own inner language can lead to new insights and change in actions.

SUMMARY OF BECOMING FRIENDS WITH YOURSELF

Look back over what you have learned from these exercises on appreciating, accepting, and letting go. What was your most important lesson? Take a few moments to summarize what you learned so that it will serve as a foundation for your continuing in the workshop.

II. To Be a Friend with Others

In this section, you will extend what you learned about being friends with yourself to being friends with others. In both cases, you must clear away obstacles so that you can offer your complete acceptance of both the positive and negative. As you learn to be a friend to others, you will build on the confidence you developed in becoming friends with yourself. The exercises in this section call for you to shift your spotlight of attention from yourself to others. To make this shift from the personal to the interpersonal, invoking my mantra, "Let my ego go." This is a temporary suspension of my personal agenda, but it is essential for focusing my attention on accepting others. Here are the exercises:

6. Recalling Being Completely Accepted
7. Recalling Being Cut Off From Friends
8. Making Space for Others
9. Accepting Differences in Others
10. Accepting Others with No Hidden Agenda

The purpose of this section is to enable you to be a friend with all others, not only those close to you. These exercises invite you to consider being a friend with anyone you choose, including strangers, acquaintances, and even those with whom you strongly disagree. To know that you can be a friend to anyone does not mean that you will be offering your friendship to everyone you meet. It means that you can choose to offer your friendship, and that you recognize that everyone needs a friend, and that your choice is not limited to those like yourself. That you can choose to be friends with anyone in the world is precious, since it also means that you can be friends with the world. And these days, the world certainly needs a friend.

Learning to be a friend with others is based on the Golden Rule of Friendship: may I be a friend to others as I would have them be a friend to me. The initial exercises help you identify the meaning of "as I would have them be a friend to me." Recalling your own experience of being accepted, as well your experience of being cut off from friends, allows you to express what it means to you to be a friend. Bringing out your personal meaning of acceptance in friendship will serve as your action guide for following the Golden Rule of Friendship.

The underlying principle in this section is accepting the humanity in every person, no matter how different they are and no matter how much you disagree with them. They are like you: they are human. Simple as it seems, this principle is often the most difficult to accept, and each of us will grasp it in our own personal way. In this section, you will find specific exercises focusing on certain features of accepting the humanity in others. After recalling your positive and negative experiences with friendship, you are invited to consider the importance of making space for the other person by clearing away your personal concerns.

Next, you consider the challenge of accepting differences in others, as well as accepting people who are entirely different. Meeting this challenge calls for overcoming the tendency to consider only people who are like ourselves as potential friends. Finally, you are invited to understand and apply the idea of accepting others with no hidden agenda or concerns about what's in it for you: to accept ... that's all.

EXERCISE 6:
RECALLING BEING COMPLETELY ACCEPTED

Based on the Golden Rule of Friendship, this exercise invites you to recall what it felt like to be completely accepted in order to identify and describe how you want to be treated as a friend. Your description of how you want to be treated as a friend will provide a personal guide for being a friend to others. By reversing roles and imagining that you are your companion offering complete acceptance, you will be following the Golden Rule of Friendship.

Attention

Think back over recent friendship experiences and identify a situation when you were with a companion in whose company you felt completely accepted. Select a situation in which you felt very comfortable and could be yourself.

Awareness

1. Take a few moments to recall your chosen situation in as much detail as possible. Close your eyes and recall what it was like: how you felt at the time, what was said, and as much as you can about what happened.

2. Open your eyes and jot down the highlights of the situation. Don't worry about the order, just list the main features that you remembered.

3. Holding these highlights in mind, try to describe why you felt so accepted. Describe the reason for the feeling of acceptance: How do you understand or make sense of this situation? What was there about your companion or yourself that led to your feeling accepted? Summarize why and how it happened.

Translate your summary into action language that expresses what you need to create this feeling of complete acceptance in others. Focus on the most important feature and express it as an action guide, which summarizes this central belief about being a friend to others.

Action

Over the next few days, try to follow your action guide in appropriate situations. Take note of what happens — how you feel about being a friend, and how it influences what happens.

HOW THIS EXERCISE WORKED FOR A PARTICIPANT

Here's an example of a participant's experience with this exercise, using a situation where she felt very comfortable and really accepted — totally herself:

Highlights of Accepted Experience

- It was a relaxed evening on a warm summer night, after dinner and a few drinks
- It was exciting just talking about anything — we couldn't stop
- There was a mutual sharing of personal life experiences, including sad ones
- Being able to express the sadness, happiness and laughter
- Feeling of "home" — it seemed to be mutual
- It was nice when this new friend felt so at home later in the evening that he found the espresso and made us both some coffee

- The flow between us was smooth and easy — it felt natural

Why Did You Feel so Accepted?

- A mutual openness and willingness to be so
- A mutual interest in each other fundamentally
- A curiosity and mutual exploration
- Everything was mutual at some level — we didn't want it to stop
- There were no expectations or demands
- There was sense of freedom and compassion in its simplicity

Action Guide:

What was the secret of the success — the essence of creating acceptance?

- Establishing a mutual match between you and someone else (or finding the match) — not worrying about anything else — what people think or don't think, do or should not do, etc.
- To let go and just be yourself completely — vulnerable — then you are at home with yourself, which invites the other to be at home with themselves and with

you. You can then share just "being" while being together
- Cherishing the simplicity of the chemistry and joy that two people can have together at the moment in time
- Thinking as an explorer

EXERCISE 7:
RECALLING BEING CUT OFF FROM FRIENDS

This exercise aims to extend your understanding of how you want to be treated as a friend by focusing on a negative experience with friendship. Even though this might be challenging and sometimes painful, you will learn as much or more by reviewing difficult situations as from positive experiences. By recalling experiences in which you felt disconnected from friendship you can explore how it feels to be cut off from friendship, as well as why this disconnection occurred. Try to blend your understanding of the negative with your reflections on the positive.

Attention

Think back over the last few months and select a situation in which you were cut off from friendship. It may be a specific situation with a companion or it may be a general feeling of being disconnected. The central

---

feature of the situation could be your feeling of disconnection from friends.

Awareness

1. Take a few moments to recall this situation in as much detail as possible. Close your eyes and recall what it was like, how you felt at the time, what was said, and as much as you can about what happened.

2. Open your eyes and jot down the highlights of the situation. Don't worry about the order, just list the main features that you remembered.

3. Holding these highlights in mind, try to describe first how you felt at the time and then try to analyze why it happened. Use your analysis to summarize what is needed to prevent this from happening again. Express, in your own words, what was missing from this experience so that you can better understand how to avoid it in the future.

Using your understanding of why this happened and what is needed to prevent its future occurrence, translate your suggestion into an action guide for being a friend. As you do so, compare this action guide with the one you developed the last exercise; note the similarity.

Action

Over the next few days, try to follow your action guide for being a friend at appropriate situations. Also take note of any times when you feel rejected or not accepted as a friend to consider these situations.

How This Exercise Worked for Me

This was a difficult exercise for me, probably because, like everyone, I am very sensitive to rejection. I have discovered that sometimes the feeling of being cut off is momentary and may pass quickly, while in other situations, my disconnected feeling is longer lasting. Recalling specific situations led to some valuable insights.

This specific focus helped me realize that I sometimes interpret disagreements with other people as personal criticism, non-acceptance, or even rejection. As the manager of the band I also play in, I am responsible for preparing a weekly musical program, and when a fellow musician disagrees or complains about a selection, I often take it it as a personal rebuff. The feeling is short-lived, but it is there. Realizing this helped me distinguish between acceptance and agreement (Exercises 9 focuses on this distinction). Since I became aware of the need to distinguish acceptance and agreement from my own failure, I tried to live by it — even though it is much more difficult to live this belief than to write about it.

When I started to pay attention to my reaction to feeling disconnected or rejected, I remembered becoming short of breath. It was as if I had been cut off from my air supply. To protect myself, I sometimes retaliated by snubbing the person, either by remaining silent or by leaving the scene entirely. In creating my shell of self-protection to deflect any further rejection, I was also trying to maintain control of the situation. What I learned from these situations, which fortunately are not all that frequent, was that being a friend means letting go of control. Again, to "accept ... that's all."

EXERCISE 8:
MAKING SPACE FOR THE OTHERS

Making mental space to welcome a friend is one of the most important, yet least appreciated, principles of learning to be a friend. When you are preoccupied by your own concerns, you are completely full of yourself, and have neither the space nor the desire to give anyone your attentive acceptance. Even when you are aware of its importance, it is not always easy to remember to clear away your own concerns each time you want to accept another person.

Self-absorption blocks communication, as well as friendly acceptance, and there are countless examples of this phenomenon. How many experts in the helping professions fail to connect with their patients because of their self-absorption and occasional narcissism? How many programs about increasing listening skills fall short because they fail to recognize the principle that you cannot listen attentively when you are preoccupied by your own concerns? You need to learn to make space for another if you want to be a friend.

You have already begun learning how to make space through two of the exercises in the previous section. By learning to identify your beliefs in Exercise 3, you are better able to set them aside to make space for the other. Setting your beliefs aside also serves to alleviate any concerns you might have about how your beliefs may be threatened by opposing beliefs. The focus on letting go in Exercise 5 is equally helpful because you make space for the other by letting your go of your ego.

It is easy to accept my words about the importance of making mental space, but actually doing so calls for a personal desire to accept the other.

Are you genuinely interested in welcoming the other person? Are you eager to learn more about the person? When you recalled being completely accepted in Exercise 6, did you feel that your friend had created a welcoming space for you? Was your experience of being accepted or cut off related to the other person's making space or crowding you out? You can best appreciate the importance of making space by recalling its significance in instances in which you received space and felt completely accepted. Applying the Golden Rule of Friendship may help you clarify your intentions so that when you take the time and effort to make space for the other it is authentic and honest. When you are genuinely devoted to being a friend, when you embrace the Spirit of Friendship, your whole-hearted commitment to living your beliefs develops a life of its own. Of course, you will be encouraged when the person shows appreciation and responds to the space you have made for them, but whatever the other's response, you will feel confident in your efforts to be a friend.

Attention

Think about all the people you might see tomorrow or in the coming days, and select one of them to focus on for this exercise. You may select anyone — a family member, close friend, or someone you barely know or will meet for the first time, even someone with whom you strongly disagree. Select someone to whom you would like to give your focus of attention, for whatever reason.

Awareness

In contrast to earlier exercises in which you recalled past situations, in this one you prepare for a future encounter.

---

1. Close your eyes and imagine that you are with the person. Try to focus your attention completely on this person to let them know that they are welcome and accepted. Does the other person seem comfortable with your approach? Notice if you experience any obstacles in the way of accepting them.

2. As you review this future situation, try to notice if your negative thoughts, such as if you start to wonder why you are doing this or what will the benefits be of accepting the person? Are there any other obstacles you notice?

3. If you have noticed any difficulty, what do you need to do to deal with the obstacle? Is your self-interest blocking the way of your welcoming the other? Are you concerned about your own beliefs being at risk?

4. Review your insights about any obstacles and develop plans to overcome these obstacles. Develop one or two action guides to follow when you do meet the person, in order to make space for them and accept them as a friend.

Action

When you meet the person, try to follow your personal guide to make space for them and then record what happens. In earlier workshops, participants who tried to change their actions often reported that this change evoked curiosity from the other person who wondered why they were behaving differently. This is the first sign that you are on the right track.

How This Exercise Worked for Me

I mentioned earlier how I found the image of being a host and the musical mantra to "let my ego go" were very helpful as I learned to make space for the other person. As I apply this principle to my daily life, I have found that its value increases. Sometimes, even when the other person is not very responsive, I learn more about them. At other times, when my companion reciprocates by making space for me, our mutual openness brings a strengthening of our friendship tie and a deepening appreciation of one another.

Initially, I thought about making space as moving from *me* to *us*. However, this omits an important step. As the three sections of this workshop show, the shift is from *me* in the first section to *you* in the second section to *we* in the third section. As I shift from *me* to *you*, the spotlight illuminates *you*, but the *me* does not disappear. Rather, my awareness of my beliefs provides a solid foundation for moving on to focus on *you*. Even so, I always experience some tension between focusing on *me* and focusing on *you*. I can describe the shifting from *me* to *you* in ideal terms, such as a switch of spotlight focus; but in practice, the *me* is never completely out of the light. The tension of focusing on *me* versus *you* is at the heart of being a friend and especially in creating the *we* of friendship ties. For now, I emphasize focusing on the *you*.

EXERCISE 9:
ACCEPTING DIFFERENCES IN OTHERS

In his 1992 book *Blue Highways*, William L. Heat-Moon describes his odyssey through the United States during which he had a conversation with an older woman who lived on an island. "What's the hardest part of living on a small, marshy island in Chesapeake Bay?" he asked. She replied, "I know that and it didn't take me sixty-three years to figure it out. Here it is wrapped up like a parcel. Listen to my sentence. Having the gumption to live different and the sense to let everybody else live different. That's the hardest thing, hands down."

This exercise focuses on the "hardest thing": to accept differences in others, both small differences in others, as well as people who are entirely different from ourselves. The difficulty comes from our tendency to focus only on ways in which others are like ourselves: similar in background, language, occupation, and so forth. It is as if we were pulled by a similarity-seeking magnet specifically designed to reveal only similarities. The more similarities we discover between ourselves and others, the better we understand them and the more comfortable we feel being with them. This similarity-seeking habit satisfies our ego's need for reassurance and control, but we pay a price for ignoring others' differences. Learning to accept the differences helps you appreciate the other person more completely: they might be different from you in some respects, but like you in other ways. Paying attention to the differences in others expands your own perspective, opening new opportunities for your development and growth. Ironically, when I take the time to try to accept the other person's differences, I often discover that we are similar in more than our underlying humanity.

To accept differences in others calls for overcoming the strong inclination to view the world only through your own image and imagining that everyone else is either like you, or could be. I became aware of this tendency while teaching a course in learning styles a few years ago. Such courses usually group students into similar learning style groups, but students in my course were surprised not to be placed in such a group. I had observed that emphasizing only similarities made it less likely that they would appreciate others with different learning styles. In fact, when surrounded only by students who learned in the same way, they tended to regard all others as inferior.

Since my aim in this course was to help them improve communication by becoming aware of all ways of learning, I used a different approach. Rather than grouping according to similarity, I grouped them in pairs with a person of an opposite learning style, with instructions to work together on a task. A student whose learning style was highly organized and who like to follow directions was paired with a student who preferred to leap into a problem to find out what happened. A student who was guided by emotional cues was paired with one who was guided by logic and rationality. It was an exercise in enforced acceptance of differences since they all directly experienced each other's very different learning styles. Students were initially surprised to observe that a style completely different from their own seemed to work reasonably well for their partner, and most were able to accept it. It may seem a modest aim, but their learning to accept differences in others was my major goal in the course, because it set the foundation for transferring their insight to other circumstances, which would then help them to be a friend.

The present exercise is similar to the learning style exercise, except that in this case, I cannot pair you with an opposite partner to maximize your focus on differences. You will be responsible for shifting your focus to the differences in other people. The purpose of this exercise is to expand your awareness of how others are different and to consider the meaning of these differences so that you can understand and accept them. It is important to emphasize again that the purpose is neither to pay attention only to differences nor to try to take in every single difference. You are simply asked to include the question, "How is this person different?" in your thinking so that you can use it to guide your actions when you choose to do so. Notice what happens when you focus on the question, "How did you feel and what did you learn?"

As you try this way of focusing, you will probably notice that accepting differences varies by situations. It is easier to accept a small difference than a large one, for example; it is also easier to accept a difference in someone with whom you have already established a similarity. The most difficult circumstance combines these two in a person with whom you strongly disagree and with whom you have very few similarities. You may initially find that it is easier to identify and consider differences after meeting the person than during. In any case, you will evolve your own techniques for accepting differences in others.

The most important point to remember is that you can accept a person without necessarily agreeing with them: acceptance does not mean agreement. It is not an easy distinction to make, but it is essential that you accept others who are different from yourself as you learn to be a friend. This exercise is intended to raise your awareness of differences in others, no matter how well you know them or how much you agree with them.

Attention

Sharpen your attention to differences by imagining that you possess a difference-seeking magnet designed to reveal differences in others. You follow this magnet by focusing on the question, "How is this person different from me?" Notice how it feels to emphasize differences as compared with previously only emphasizing similarities.

Awareness

1. Take a few minutes to recall a recent encounter with another person who was different from yourself. Close your eyes to recall the situation as clearly as possible. You were probably unaware of the difference at the time, but focus on the question, "How is this person different?"

2. Jot down your observations about the person's differences and compare them with their similarities.

3. Review how you have accepted the person's differences and similarities, and consider how expanding your acceptance to their differences helped you understand the person more clearly. Regardless of whether

or not you agree with them, do you feel you know them better now?

4. What are the implications of your impressions? What have you learned from this emphasis on differences? Does it seem worthwhile? If so, describe your own action guide for detecting and accepting differences.

Action

During the next few days, apply your action guide for accepting differences in appropriate situations. If possible, apply it to someone very different from you to test how far you can extend your acceptance.

HOW THIS EXERCISE WORKED FOR ME

I find it is much easier to write about accepting differences than to put it into practice. My experience of trying to accept differences was very similar to my reaction to recalling being cut off in Exercise 7: I tend to interpret differences as possible rejection. But from this exercise, I have learned that it is the unexpected differences that are the most difficult to accept. When I meet a new person, I expect there to be many differences between us, and I am prepared to accept them, at least initially. However, it's always surprising when a family member or close friend expresses a new belief that seems totally out of character. I have discovered that dealing with such unexpected differences is one of the biggest challenges to being a friend: it means that I need to change as well in order to sustain and strengthen our friendship tie. I must focus on the underlying trust that binds our friendship as I accept my friend's newly expressed and unexpected difference.

When I meet someone for the first time I have fewer expectations, so I can more easily be open and accepting of them, despite our differences. When trying to accept differences in people that I already know, it is more difficult because I often rehearse our meetings beforehand in my mind so that any deviations from my anticipated script become difficult to accept. (Since all of the exercises are interrelated, the one that follows is about how to shed your expectations so that you can better accept the other.)

I wish I could say that I have been able to accept some people who are completely different from me, because that is the true test of accepting the other's humanity. However, the closest I have come is remaining in conversation with someone with whom I disagree only to find out that we did agree on something. For example, I was talking to a psychotherapist whose approach I strongly disagreed with, but as we spoke I discovered that he enjoyed music, giving us a common interest that made the difference seemed less predominant.

I need to explain why I take the time to write about accepting those with whom I completely disagree when I have not been able to fully practise the belief myself. I include this topic because I think that in today's world of increasing conflict we need to begin trying to accept the basic humanity of those with whom we disagree. Otherwise, the strength of these disagreements can only have devastating consequences.

I conclude this exercise with the often-quoted comments by the poet, Rilke, in *Dragons into Princesses*:

> We have no reason to mistrust our world, for it is not against us. Has it terrors, they are our terrors; has it abysses, those abysses belong to us; are dangers at hand, we must try and love them. And if only we arrange our life according to that principle which counsels us that we must always hold to the difficult, then that which now still seems to us the most alien will become what we most trust and find most faithful.
>
> How should we be able to forget those ancient myths that are at the beginning of all peoples, the myths about dragons that at the last moment turn into princesses; perhaps all the dragons of our lives are princesses who are only waiting to see us once beautiful and brave. Perhaps everything terrible is in its deepest being something helpless that needs our love.

EXERCISE 10:
ACCEPTING OTHERS WITH NO HIDDEN AGENDA

When considering your experience of complete acceptance, as you did in Exercise 6, don't you find it to be true that your friend's acceptance was also completely unselfish, with no hidden agenda? I can't emphasize this enough: unselfish acceptance is one of the most important features of being a friend. Therefore, you must also set aside your personal needs to clarify your intentions of being a friend. Whether this means suspending your personal agenda, or letting your ego go as I like to think of it, you need to develop your own words to help you set aside your self-interest. This exercise aims to help you learn to accept a person purely because you want to be a friend, nothing more.

There are many ways to accept and offer friendship. You may simply smile and greet the person, you may listen attentively, you may offer your help, or give a gift. Whatever your actions, your motivation needs to be friendship and nothing more. Suspending your personal agenda allows you to clearly focus your attention on the other person. Although you have set aside the expectation of a response to your acceptance, and will appreciate your friend's reciprocation, it is not the purpose of your actions. If decide to offer help to someone, do so only because you want to be helpful. If you offer a gift, do so only because you feel like giving something to this person. Your aim in being a friend is to convey your heartfelt intention as

purely as possible, and the better you are at suspending your expectations and self-interest, the better
you can communicate your friendship.

As you engage in this exercise you will become
aware of your own intentions in offering your
friendship and you may be surprised. Sometimes
hidden agendas pop up where you least expect
them.

Friendship flourishes when both parties accept
each other in a Spirit of Friendship. I hope that this
exercise in unselfish acceptance you will help you
begin to sense friendship's magic.

Attention

Select a particular act of acceptance to focus
on. Then, consider your past experience with
several ways of being a friend: (1) greeting
the person with a smile, (2) listening attentively, (3) offering to help, or (4) giving a gift.
Pay attention to your experience with one
of these. If you focus on offers of help, for
example, try to recall the various situations in
which you have recently offered.

Awareness

1. Recall an experience you've had of
   accepting another as completely as
   possible. Close your eyes and try to

---

recall as much as possible about your feelings, what went on, and how the other person responded.

2. Jot down the highlights of your experience, especially your thoughts before and after.

3. Describe why you wanted to accept this person and how you felt about what happened.

4. Develop a plan of action based on your experience which will allow you to accept with no expectations. Try to express it as an action guide in your own words.

Action

Try out your action plan in an appropriate situation. Pay attention to your motivation and how you feel about the other person's response. Notice any differences you feel in suspending your expectations. If this is your first time, it may be difficult and you may want to try this several times.

HOW THIS EXERCISE WORKED FOR ME

You've already heard my personal action guide, which developed from this exercise: "Accept … that's all." It evolved from my experience giving gifts, when I realized that sometimes my intent was to bring attention to myself rather than to show my friendship. Therefore, "that's all" means that my motivation is not any kind of hidden motive. It is to be a friend, that's all. Somehow, these two words shut the door on anything other than my initial purpose to be a friend. That is my purpose, *bang*: no other purposes allowed.

It works especially well when I greet someone, in case they don't respond. After some practise, I find that I am unconcerned whether they respond or not, since my intention in saying, "Good morning," was simply to communicate that we are sharing the day. This action guide also works for the previous exercise about accepting differences. In that case, "that's all" means that I do not have to agree to accept a person's differences. I will describe my experience with "accept ... that's all" in more detail in a later chapter.

For now I want to clarify that although to "accept ... that's all" may sound abrupt, its meaning depends on my emphasis on the word *accept*. The word "that's" does not carry a negative emphasis; rather it helps me accept. As with all action guides, it is only in applying them that I can learn their meaning.

I would like to conclude this section on the importance of accepting the humanity of others with the example of one of my best friend's who spent five years in a Japanese prison camp during the Second World War. Even while experiencing almost unendurable suffering, he thought of his captors as like him in that they were also in the army, following orders, and away from their families. He disagreed with them completely but he tried to accept them as being human like himself … that's all.

III. To Strengthen Your Friendship Ties

Throughout our lives, we develop many friendship ties with others, especially family members and close friends, and these friendships give meaning to our lives. Nothing is more important than our friendship ties, yet we often take them for granted. This section offers exercises to encourage you to focus attention on your friendship ties, to discover what they need and how you can strengthen them:

11. Appreciating Your Friendship As It Is Today
12. Imagining Your Friendship As It Might Be
13. Appreciating Your Friend's Heart's Desire
14. Choosing Your Actions to Strengthen Friendship Ties
15. Honouring the Spirit of Friendship

Let's begin with a brief discussion of friendship ties. I like to think of my connection to others as friendship ties rather than relationships, although both terms are accurate. The phrase *friendship ties* conveys a heartfelt and personal connection while the term *relationship* seems abstract and impersonal. I also like the image of a tie of friendship that can vary from the small connection of one tiny thread to a much deeper connection of a woven tapestry of trust.

Imagining your connections as friendship ties offers a way of visualizing how the threads of your interactions with your friends gradually weave a strong fabric of trust.

Friendship ties are based on the interlocking expectations that develop gradually through the back-and-forth of your encounters. These interlocking expectations define your friendships and how you will interact with one another. A simple example: you may come to expect that your companion will take the lead in conversation and your companion may come to expect that you will respond in certain ways. As a result of many such encounters, you and your friend gradually develop a feeling of trust that is the essence of friendship.

As your expectations for one another develop, this evolving feeling of trust develops a life of its own and becomes a tapestry of trust. The underlying sense of trust of your friend is the invisible presence — the Spirit of Friendship — which guides your actions and interactions in your friendship. The stronger the tie of friendship, the more solid and dependable your sense of trust. And nothing is more important than trust in yourself and in your friends, which allow you to be open and accepting of the many changes that occur in friendships. Change is inevitable. You change or your friend changes, and your friendship itself changes. The purpose of this section is to learn to accept these changes while being supported by the underlying tie of trust. It is by accepting, even welcoming, change that your ties of friendship are freshly strengthened. When both you and your friend accept each other as you are, your tapestry of trust is woven into an even stronger fabric.

The purpose of the first exercise is to accept your friendship as it is at the present moment. Accepting your friendship in the present means that you must first become aware of your own present state and then pay particular attention to how your friend is at this time. This exercise builds upon what you did in Exercise 2 when you became aware of your personal presence.

Once you have experienced accepting your friendship as it is, the next exercise invites you to imagine how your friendship might be. Specifically, you consider the question, "What would my specific friendship be like if each of us focused on the other at their best?" This exercise emphasizes an important role of friendship: to help each other grow and develop. Friendship is the essential means of reaching our human potential and, surprisingly, you are more likely to develop your own potential when you focus on encouraging your friend's development.

Earlier exercises relied on the Golden Rule of Friendship to help you clarify your actions of being a friend. The Golden Rule is a useful but limited beginning step because not everyone wants to be treated in the same way you prefer, necessarily. Therefore, the next exercise goes beyond the Golden Rule by rephrasing it as follows: may I do unto others as they would prefer to be done unto. This rule calls for you to become specifically aware of your companion's needs and desires regarding friendship. There will likely be many features that are the same as yours, however, there may be other features that are different. You may want your companion to show their acceptance with words describing how they feel toward you, while your companion may prefer simple actions. In any case, the more clearly you can appreciate your friend's personal needs and desires, the stronger will be your tie of friendship.

What you will learn in Exercise 13 about your friend's specific wishes for friendship will help you with Exercise 14, the purpose of which is to show you how to choose your actions to strengthen your friendship ties. You will pay attention to your friendship ties by posing this question before you act: "Will my actions strengthen or weaken our friendship?" The more clearly you learned to appreciate your friend's view of friendship in Exercise 13, the better you will be able to anticipate the effect of your actions and choose those most likely to strengthen your friendship ties.

We will conclude with an exercise that might have been given an entire section of its own because of its significance: how to welcome the Spirit of Friendship. We will acknowledge that no matter how much we plan and practise to be a friend, the development of friendship is beyond our control; we cannot control the reaction of the other person, and more importantly, friendship is essentially mysterious, following a path of its own. What we can do is to try to invoke the Spirit of Friendship through our actions … that's all.

The exercises in this final section focus on your friendship ties, but they also depend on what you have learned in earlier exercises. Each exercise focuses on a specific aspect of being a friend, but the ultimate aim is to coordinate what you learn into a seamless pattern so that your being a friend becomes a habit. In order to make the exercises relevant to your daily life, I invite you to choose someone close to you so that you can focus on your friendship with this chosen friend in the exercises. You may choose a family member or a close friend, someone whose friendship you would like to explore.

EXERCISE 11:
APPRECIATING YOUR FRIENDSHIP AS IT IS TODAY

When you next meet with your friend it is like greeting the new day with its fresh possibilities. You appreciate your friendship by greeting your friend with attentive presence and openness. Imagine that you have not seen your friend for some time and want to be in touch as completely as possible. As in Exercise 2, you need to open all of your senses, as well as your heart, to your friend. Begin by opening to yourself to become aware of how you are in the moment, then turn your attention to your friend to learn how they are today. Be completely present to yourself, your friend, and your friendship as it is today.

Your attention might focus on a single question, such as, "How are you?" You need to take this cliché seriously. Paying attention to your friend in the moment is similar to your focus in Exercise 9, when you emphasized the question, "How are you different?" In this case, though, consider how your friend is different today from the last time you met. This means that your friendship has also changed, if only slightly, and you will need to accept this, even if it is difficult.

Applying the Golden Rule of Friendship may also help raise your awareness about the importance of being present to your friend in the moment. Think about your own experience with friends, those times when your current mental state was completely ignored and those times when your companion took the time to really discover how you were at that moment. One way to dramatize the importance of this exercise is to think of a conversation you might have had when something very important has just happened — a death in the family, a promotion at work, or some other big event — and the other person never gave you a chance to reveal what was important to you right then. Conversely, have you been the unconscious perpetrator in ignoring your friend's problems by going on automatic pilot without being open to how your friend was at the time?

This exercise will help you develop a personal approach to appreciating your friendship, to accepting changes in yourself, in your friend, and in your friendship. The goal is not only to accept it, but to welcome change for the rejuvenation it provides.

Attention

Throughout this exercise, your attention should focus on your chosen friend, by first recalling how your friend was at your last meeting and then, in future meetings, giving your attentive acceptance to that friend.

Awareness

1. Recall the last time you were with this person and try to remember as much as possible about your meeting. Close your eyes and recall what was said, how you felt, and what your impressions were.

2. Jot down the highlights of the remembered event. Try to recall as much as possible about your feelings and impressions.

3. How would you summarize your impressions of your friend at this time. What was on your friend's mind, did he or she have any concerns, what was your friend's mood? How much did you feel you knew about your friend at this time?

4. Based on your experience in this situation, how would you become more attentive to your friend at your next

---

meeting? Try to express this in your own words as an action guide.

Action

The next time you meet your chosen friend, try to follow your action guide to pay attention to your friend at the time. Note what happens, how you feel, and how your friend responds.

HOW THIS EXERCISE WORKED FOR ME

Some of the clearest examples I've found of the importance of accepting a friend in the moment come from telephone conversations with people with whom I haven't communicated in a while. These conversations vary greatly in terms of how much time the other person devoted to finding out how I was at the time. Some did initially focus on discovering how I was doing, but others focused only on themselves and their concerns. I always try to remember to begin every conversation by asking my friend how they are doing before we go ahead with our conversation. It's embarrassing to discover, in the middle of a conversation, that that he or she has experienced a major life problem and I'd rambled on about my own problems.

I often wonder why some friendship ties remain strong over the years while others weaken. If you have been to a school reunion, perhaps your experience was similar to mine: I discovered that some of my friendship ties were still strong, even though we hadn't communicated for years. Upon reflection, I realized that it was because, in our original friendship, we had each been concerned with one another and formed a trusting bond. It is a testimony to the strength of our friendship tie that it remains strong after all these years.

EXERCISE 12:
IMAGINING YOUR FRIENDSHIP AS IT MIGHT BE

Friendship is a precious gift in so many ways, yet its most important benefit is often least appreciated. That is, being a friend is your best opportunity to realize the human potential in both your friend and yourself. Friendship holds the key to transforming the abstract goal of potential into the reality of becoming what we may be by throwing all of your energy and attention into encouraging your friends to grow and develop. By choosing to encourage your friend's development, you are unknowingly developing your capacity to help others: you are becoming what you may be.

This exercise offers you an opportunity to discover the surprising consequences of focusing on what you and your friend may be. It is a guided imagery exercise that invites you to visit a Magical Pool, which reflects you at your best and as you might be and allows you to glimpse the possibilities of human potential for both you and your friend. After you have explored the Magical Pool on your own, you invite your chosen friend to join you as you each discover how your friendship might be if you each encouraged each other to be at your best.

Attention

Guided imagery usually involves two people, one who guides and one who imagines, but in this case you will need to play both roles (unless you have chosen to work with a partner). You can act as your own guide by reading through the instructions once or twice so that you can follow them without relying on the book. Then shift your role and imagine that you are at the Magical Pool. If you find that you need to shift back to check on the instructions, that's fine.

Awareness

Imagine that you are walking through a beautiful forest, along an inviting path. Open yourself to all of the forest — not only what it looks like and sounds like, but also its smell and what it feels like. Enjoy your walk.

Up ahead you notice a body of water that seems to call to you, so you walk over to investigate. You discover that it is a beautiful

---

pool, and you soon discover that it is not an ordinary pool that simply reflects your image like a mirror, but a Magical Pool. Its magic is its capacity to reveal your hidden qualities and capabilities: to show you yourself at your very best.

This is an exciting prospect, so you sit at the edge of the pool and gaze into it. It may reveal your hidden qualities as words or you may see yourself reflected as an image of these qualities. Focus on the pool and notice what bubbles up.

As you become aware of some of your usually hidden capabilities, consider how you feel about them and what you might like to do about it. How does it make you feel?

Since you have enjoyed this experience, you decide to share it with a companion: your chosen friend. Your friend comes down the path to join you and you invite him or her to look into the Magical Pool. Each of you spends some time viewing your own reflections. You invite your companion to look at your magical reflection and become aware of you at your best. Both of you take a few moments to consider your hidden qualities.

Next, you both look at your companion's hidden qualities and discuss them. You tell your companion your reaction — surprise, delight, whatever. Then finally, you both look into the Magical Pool again and consider what your relationship would be like if each of you were at your best and if each of you acknowledged the hidden positive qualities within the other.

Take some time to talk and compare your relationship as it is revealed by the Magical Pool with your relationship as it is.

It is time to leave so you walk back up the path through the woods again. On completing your visit, take a few moments to record your experience at the Magical Pool with an emphasis on how you can apply it in your relationship with your close friend.

Action

Next time you meet your chosen friend, focus on your friend's best qualities and try to encourage these. Continue to nurture your friend's development. You might even describe the Magical Pool to your friend and ask them if they would also like to use it to encourage your friendship to become what it might be.

HOW THIS EXERCISE WORKED FOR PARTICIPANTS

Here is an example of one participant's experience at the Magical Pool:

I looked into the pool and saw my reflection. I saw the qualities of optimism, humour, love of family and job expertise surrounding my reflection. It took a little while for these to be easily seen. Initially the water was brown and murky when I was guided to think about hidden qualities, but eventually the water cleared to reveal these things.

Then I brought my husband to the pool. He came over and sat on a fallen log beside the pool. I moved from the rock, and sat beside him on the log. We both looked into the pool, and I looked at his reflection. When I began looking for his hidden qualities the water became murky again, but suddenly there were many ripples in the water surrounding his reflection. Some of the qualities in these ripples were loyalty, sense of humour, family dedication and friendship. We spent the rest of the time in companionable silence, reflecting on our images in the pool.

Reaction to the exercise: I was surprised at the emotions that I experienced with this exercise. When I looked at my husband's reflection, I felt a sense of sadness and regret. The exercise made me realize that I don't spend any time reflecting on his good qualities. I didn't feel any emotions when considering my own hidden qualities, although it took a little time for them to be clearly seen.

Clearly, this exercise raised the participant's awareness about the value of opening up to her husband's good qualities, which requires her to let go of fixed perceptions.

Here is another example, this time from a husband becoming aware of his wife:

> My experience consisted of seeing many qualities that I would like to integrate in to my life and in myself. Qualities such as patience, expressiveness, unconditional love, and acceptance. My experience also consisted of inviting my wife to the pool. What I found when looking for qualities for her to integrate was that she currently possesses the very qualities I want to incorporate into my being. When I began to imagine what our relationship would be like with the implementation of these qualities I saw two people who were happy and content.
>
> Reflections: As a result of this exercise, I have been consistently thinking about and looking for opportunities to incorporate these qualities in my life. It has not been difficult to find opportunities where I experience myself shutting down emotionally, becoming frustrated, and/or experiencing a lack of patience. I have also felt challenged by my urge to use my old less effective method of "conditional love" or control. I have discussed with my

wife as to how we might improve our communication and relationship.

In this case, the new awareness led directly to action, which is the best possible result of the exercise.

Sometimes, the companion at the Magical Pool is not the person expected, as the following example illustrates:

As I listened to the instructions for this exercise, I decided to ask my husband to join me at the pool. My intention was to reflect upon our relationship and some of its specific qualities. The walk through the woods to the pool had a mysterious, almost surreal quality to it, something like a Rousseau painting. Each detail was precise and shiny. There were huge ferns with dark glossy leaves. The earth smelled pungent, and the ground was soft under my feet. The path seemed to draw me down it, as if something special were waiting for me at the end. I had a feeling of excited anticipation.

The pool was a surprise, totally different in atmosphere to the path. Whereas the path had been dark and mysterious, the pool was light and clear. Sunlight found its way through the trees. There were reeds and rushes and a small clearing where I knelt down and could see my reflection in the water. The qualities I wanted to reflect upon were warmth, outgoingness and openness. I looked in the water and saw myself at different stages in my life, the slight ripples of the water seeming to expand my vision and my qualities, allowing them to become more defined, and yet at the same time more free. As I stared into the water, reflected back at me was a warm, open woman, myself at my best, and as I would always like to be.

I walked back along the path, feeling light and joyful, expecting to find my husband waiting for me. Instead my mother was standing at a bend in the path. When I asked her why she was there she did not answer, but took my hand and led me back to the pool. We stared into the water which no longer gave back a clear reflection. Strong ripples obscured what had previously been easy to see. I started to talk about my qualities of warmth and openness and why I found it so hard to share them with her. Our debate turned to the critical aspect of her relationship with me and why she found it so difficult to express her own warmth. As we talked it seemed that we both opened to really hear the other. The water gradually became less rippled until I could see our reflection quite clearly. Then my mother sort of faded away and was replaced by my son. He continued my conversation with my mother and I felt myself "becoming" my mother and talking as if I were her. I heard him respond as if it were myself talking. The pool remained calm enough to reflect back the qualities of my mother-myself, and myself-my son, relationship.

If self-knowledge is a prerequisite for change, I believe that this exercise helped me to take a step in that direction. Through the rippled cloudiness of the Magical Pool I was able to see the reflection of the similarities in two mother-child relationships. The decision to change my relationship with my son is at least partially up to me. I feel more confident in my ability to make changes. I feel more in control.

Notice that when "when we both opened to really hear each other," the pool cleared and the revelations began. This also shows the value of letting go of the original expectation of what she thought she would be sharing with her husband. This example runs the gamut from letting go to opening up to taking action. It also shows how the world of imagery is not always logical, but it does reveal what is in your heart.

EXERCISE 13:
APPRECIATING YOUR FRIEND'S HEART'S DESIRE

In this exercise, you will continue to focus on your chosen friend and build on your experience at the Magical Pool.

Through the reflections of the Magical Pool, you became aware of the value of accepting both your and your friend's potential, which is also about appreciating your friend's heart's desire. Since friendship allows you to encourage your friend to develop his or her potential, when you focus your attention on your friend's heart's desire, you will gradually become aware of a feeling of rightness. This is because you are simultaneously moving closer to your own heart's desire: to be a friend. No wonder it feels right!

This exercise invites you to extend your definition of friendship to include your friend's heart's desires. Here you will attentively accept and encourage your friend's development so that the friendship can flourish, much as it did from what you saw in your visit to the Magical Pool.

You will also focus your attention on your friend to learn as much as possible about his or her desires, outlook on life, and concerns. In this case, attentive acceptance means to shift your attention as completely as possible to fully appreciate your friend. Here is an example: A friend of mine, who is a very talented painter, told me the story of how he learned how different people viewed his paintings. When my friend showed one of his paintings to a colleague, the colleague confessed that he was colour-blind and unable to fully appreciate the painting. Interestingly enough, there is a software program that has a lens on it that reveals exactly how a colour-blind person sees things. Using a split screen, my friend could display how his painting looked to normal viewers on the left-hand side and, on the right, how his painting looked to the colour-blind. This story provides a useful image for this exercise: discovering the personal lens through which your friend views the world.

Each of us brings our own unique lens to view our world: there may be similarities between your view and your friend's view, as well as in your desires, but each is distinct. To appreciate your friend's heart's desire, you need to go beyond the Golden Rule of Friendship. You need to pose the question, "What does my friend want?"

You glimpsed the importance of your differences in Exercise 9, but you need to build on what you learned there. This exercise extends your learning to include both your awareness of your friend's intentions and your own. I imagine that my friendship is guided by an invisible presence between us, a presence that contains each of our intentions as well as our perception of each other's intentions. The more accurately each of us appreciates the other's intentions the better. It is also true that we need a trusting climate to reveal our heart's desires because doing so makes us quite vulnerable. And as our friendship grows, the tapestry of trust becomes stronger and we are more willing to reveal our heart's desires.

Attention

Focus your attention on your chosen friend and the question, "What does my friend want?" both when you are together and between visits, so that you can reflect on the question properly.

Awareness

Try to raise your awareness of your friend's heart's desire by reflecting on your own desires, even though these might not be the same. This allows you to appreciate how your desires influence your outlook and your actions. By beginning with yourself you can appreciate that it is not always easy to describe your heart's desire in specific terms.

Nevertheless, use your reflection to consider your friend. What is it that makes your friend happy? What is it that makes your friend smile? The answer may be their family, their job, an avocation, or hobby. What is most important in your friend's life?

Trying to answer these questions requires you to completely focus on your friend. Notice how your friend reacts to different things, including what you say to discern your friend's desires. Give him or her your complete attention without any pressure, simply taking your friend in as completely as possible.

When you have formed an impression of your friend's heart's desire, if only what makes your friend smile, then use your appreciation to develop an action guide.

Action

Using your awareness as a gentle guide, focus your actions on accepting your friend's desires. It is important that your encouragement be woven into your natural reaction to your friend so that it is doesn't seem like an unnatural attempt to manipulate and control them. Notice how you feel taking this action and how your friend responds.

How This Exercise Worked for Me

My work as a psychologist has been guided by my belief in human potential. But, I was not been so successful in some of my earlier efforts to understand and encourage this potential. I always knew that following our heart's desire was important to reaching our potential, but this seemed abstract and obvious. It was when I realized that being a friend held the key to human potential that everything fell into place. First, I realized that by appreciating my friend's heart's desire it would encourage them reaching their full potential. But it was also the realization that encouraging them was also the key to developing my own potential. It is a surprising example of the mysterious workings of the Spirit of Friendship that by shifting my focus away from myself to the other person, I found the key to my personal development.

My work supervising graduate students in planning and conducting their doctoral theses is a clear example of how I have tried to encourage other people's heart's desires. In helping them select the subject of their doctoral theses, I encouraged them to reflect on their own personal experiences to discern what they believe to be most important: their heart's desire. In psychology, the opportunity to do research, especially a doctoral thesis, is an opportunity to expand one's own understanding and beliefs about human affairs. When students identified what was most personally important to them about their topic, they not only became much more motivated, but they were more knowledgeable in the subject.

Students' desires varied widely, from the expression of empathy to working together in groups to evoking musical creativity in their subjects. Whatever it was, my intent was to appreciate their desire and encourage its development. Even though it was an academic setting, their struggle to find and follow their desires was similar to my struggle to find my own desires in my personal life. They each experienced initial difficulty in identifying their desire and, once it was identified, felt unsure about its acceptability as a thesis topic. For my part, I felt a certain confidence in encouraging them. I was pleased to see them develop and grow, and even more pleased in many case when we became friends.

EXERCISE 14:
CHOOSING YOUR ACTIONS
TO STRENGTHEN FRIENDSHIP TIES

This exercise is based on the question, "Will my actions strengthen or weaken my friendship ties?" The question seems straightforward, but applying it is challenging: it not only tests how much you actually value your friendship, but also depends on an awareness of the effects of your actions on your friend. This question is the ultimate test of being a friend and covers three related issues: how important your friendship is to you; how will your friend feel and respond to your actions; and, if you think that your actions are likely to weaken your friendship ties, how can you learn to change them?

You will begin to explore the value you place on friendship, as compared to your many other desires, by thinking about how your actions will affect others throughout the day. You will need to put yourself in your friend's position in order to appreciate his or her feelings and outlook on life so that you can anticipate the effect of your actions, which builds on what you learned in the last exercise.

We have already considered a few actions that are likely to strengthen your friendships, such as listening attentively, helping, and giving gifts, but you need to consider the specific situation before assuming that taking one of these actions will strengthen your friendship. And the most crucial situation in which you must concern yourself with the affects of your actions is when you are responding directly to your friend. If your words may hinder your friendship, it is be best to remain silent. I often recall, with admiration, how my late mother often responded when someone described their difficulties to her. With a big smile, she would respond with an extended, "Weeeeelll," which gave the other complete assurance of acceptance. Of course, she sometimes went beyond this short reply, but it was so helpful that I have tried to emulate it.

I realize that by unpacking this apparently simple question, how my actions affect others, I may have made it sound so daunting that you may be disinclined to try it. But let me conclude this introduction by emphasizing that by occasionally posing this question either before you act or in retrospect, you will become aware of yourself as a friend and that is our main purpose here.

Attention

You may initially pose this question in relation to your chosen friend by considering your past interactions: "Have my actions

---

strengthened or weakened our friendship?" The answer will serve as a basis for your thinking about the question when you next meet your chosen friend. Keep the question in mind throughout even if you aren't necessarily taking any action.

Awareness

Notice how your chosen friend responds to your various actions so that you can form a distinct impression of your friend's current outlook and circumstance. As you did in the last exercise, try to develop approaches that will enhance your friendship and increase your trust. Notice how you feel about putting the friendship first. Does it seem right for you or does it seem like a required exercise that goes against your natural instincts? Take your reactions and create an action guide so that you can be prepared for future situations.

Action

When you are with your chosen friend, try to follow this action guide as much as possible. Take note both of how your friend responds as well as how you feel about putting your friendship first.

How This Exercise Worked for Me

I know that it is essential to apply the awareness of how my actions affect my friend if I want to encourage friendship to flourish in my life, but it is nonetheless very challenging. My efforts to apply it have led to two more specific action guides.

First, I find that I listen more carefully and that I am much more likely to say nothing or agree with a short reply and a smile. Second, and closely related, I follow my personal guide to "accept ... that's all," which in this case means I want to honour my friendship by accepting my friend with no qualifications, without judging.

EXERCISE 15:
HONOURING THE SPIRIT OF FRIENDSHIP

Friendship has a life of its own, following an mysterious underlying force: the Spirit of Friendship. To be a friend you must honouring the Spirit of Friendship by trusting it, allowing it to guide your actions towards being a friend. In order to do so, you must accept that the Spirit of Friendship is always within you, ready to flow and enrich your life. Learning the various approaches suggested by the exercises is the first step, but unless you trust the Spirit of Friendship, these exercises are a waste of time. All of this takes a leap of faith and this exercise will help you learn more about trusting this mysterious inner spirit.

You can often feel the flow of friendship within yourself. This may come from acting on your beliefs or from being in touch with your friend and your tapestry of trust. Focusing on your personal friendship experiences will help you appreciate the importance of the Spirit of Friendship. Friendship is mysterious and beyond your control, not only because it has a life of its own, but also because you cannot control other people's reaction. Honouring the Spirit of Friendship means letting go of any attempt to control the flow of friendship. This does not mean abandoning the action guides in the exercise, rather it means you need to practise these guides with openness to the Spirit of Friendship.

The purpose of this exercise is to experience the underlying Spirit of Friendship, to discover that it is always there, and to trust it to guide your actions in being a friend. Since this exercise on Honouring the Spirit of Friendship is the most important of all, I placed it last: you are more likely to be aware of it after you have practised the previous guides to be a friend. Like everything in life, you learn to appreciate the mysterious Spirit of Friendship with practise.

Attention

Friendship is always flowing in various places, sometimes outside yourself, between other people, and sometimes within. Spend some time focusing on the flow of friendship in

---

your life. Focus your attention with the question, "Is friendship flowing here?"

Awareness

When you are paying attention to the flow of friendship, try to determine how you feel. Try to become aware of your personal friendship experiences, as well as the underlying spirit and feeling. Consider what it means to you to possess this inner spirit that you cannot control, but which offers enormous power.

Notice that connecting with the Spirit of Friendship involves focusing solely on your intent — to offer your friendship — not on your personal gain or the effect of your actions. Try to develop your own personal words for accepting the Spirit of Friendship, trusting it, and allowing it to guide your actions.

Action

Try to imbue your actions with the Spirit of Friendship by following your personal guide. Notice how you feel when you let go of control and accept the guidance of this Spirit. Notice also what happens when you apply it to your friendships.

HOW THIS EXERCISE WORKED FOR ME

To honour the Spirit of Friendship is to honour its mystery and has revealed it to be one of my most valuable guides. I will describe its importance in greater detail in Part 3. It is especially valuable in my work as a psychologist where I often feel pressure to fully understand another person and the reasons for their actions. When I applied the Spirit of Friendship to the challenge of deciphering why human beings act as they do, I felt enormous relief to realize that so much of human activity will always be mysterious and unfathomable. Honouring the mystery helped me accept my not knowing.

David E. Hunt

IV. Concluding Exercise

Bringing Out Your Meaning of Friendship: A Meaning Map

Finding Your Personal Guide for Being a Friend

This final exercise will help you put your beliefs about friendship into practice by fully bringing out the personal guides for being a friend that you have developed. We need personal guides to counteract the obstacles we often encounter when trying to practise our beliefs: we may be aware of our personal beliefs, but not how to express them in our actions. My solution is to think of an image, like being a host welcoming a companion into my home. When I act on my image simply by saying to myself, "If I were a host…," I am immediately guided to actions that are true to my beliefs, no longer blocked by old habits. My image of being a host, like my other images of friendship, is an indispensable guide to my ability to be a friend. In the following section, I will briefly summarize the surprising value of these guides to persuade you to find your personal guides for being a friend.

Images help express our beliefs in action language. When I say to myself, "If I were a host," it gradually changes everything: I become a host as my companion becomes my guest. Being guided by my image not only changes my actions, but my feelings and thoughts as well. Becoming a host shifts my thoughts away from the interference of old, automatic habits, which once blocked the way, leaving me free to live my beliefs. Becoming a host guides my actions in how I offer my friendship, as I make space for my companion, and make sure that my guest will be comfortable. I listen carefully and carry out new actions that arise spontaneously. I was surprised when this slight shift in my imagination opened these new possibilities that I had not anticipated. For example, I found that I become more attentive to my companion's physical comfort.

Images compress complexity. It is much easier to say to myself, "If I were a host," than to try to remember all of my complex beliefs about friendship. As an image guide, the simple word *host* contains many of my complex beliefs about friendship, which are released into action when I become a host. Becoming my image is like adding water to the capsule so that it bursts open, providing valuable guidance.

I have described my image guide to encourage you to identifying your own personal guide for being a friend. I know from my earlier workshops on imagery that your initial reaction is likely to be skeptical. You may doubt the value of images, or you may feel that you are incapable of imagination. I also know that when participants in my workshops set aside their skepticism long enough to simply try imagining, they find out just how valuable imagery can be. Even if you have not engaged actively in any of the earlier exercises, I hope you will take a leap of faith and accept my invitation to participate in this final exercise. It embodies the essence of the entire workshop: to be a friend in your own way. This exercise consists of two parts. First, you create a personal meaning map of friendship by identifying its meaning as you experience it through your senses, your feelings, your actions, and your thoughts. By considering questions such as, "How does it sound?" "What does it look like?" and "How does it feel?" you will discover your personal meaning of friendship. Your meaning map lays the foundation for the second part of the exercise in which you look over all of your associations and select one of them as the basis of your image guides. Let's begin with the meaning map.

CREATING YOUR MEANING MAP

You will need a sheet of paper for your meaning map. In the middle of the sheet, print the word *FRIENDSHIP* as the centerpiece of your map.

Attention

Take a few moments to clear your mind and focus on your friendship experiences by recalling recent situations in which you were being a friend or in touch with friendship.

Awareness

What follows are twelve different approaches to bringing out your personal meaning of friendship. You need not respond to each one, as some approaches are likely to be more helpful than others. Read through the first approach on sound, then take a few moments to consider and jot down your response on your meaning map. Do this for each step.

You may portray your meaning in words, pictures, or diagrams — it is your map. As you read the next approach, allow yourself to relax and simply free-associate to the questions. Enjoy your discoveries.

1. **SOUND.** What is the *sound* of friendship? Is there a tone of voice that reminds you of being a friend? Are there sounds in nature that you associate with friendship? What about sounds in your daily life; anything there that reminds you of being a friend? Is there a song or a musical piece that you associate with friendship? How about musical instruments?

2. **SIGHT.** What does friendship look like if you drew a picture of it or

captured it with a camera? Is there a colour of friendship? Does it have a shape or form? What would it look like on a postcard? Are there scenes from nature or your everyday life that remind you of being a friend? Are there paintings, movies, or plays that you think of when you think of friendship?

3. **TOUCH.** What is the texture of friendship? Soft, smooth, rough? What would it feel like on your fingertips or the pores of your skin? How could you detect it by touching?

4. **SMELL.** What is the smell of friendship? How could you detect it with your nose? Does it have a special aroma or scent? Are there certain smells in nature that remind you of friendship?

5. **TASTE.** How might friendship taste? Sour, sweet, salty? Are there any foods or dishes that seem related to friendship? How would you capture friendship with your taste buds?

6. **FEELING.** Now let's turn to your feelings. What does it feel like to be a friend? Imagine you are in touch with

your friend, how does this feel? How would you describe your experience of friendship through your emotions?

7. **BODY SENSATIONS.** Also related are your bodily sensations when you are being a friend. How do you experience friendship in your body — in your throat, muscles, stomach, skin, bones? Where does it seem to be located? What is your bodily experience when you are being a friend?

8. **ACTION.** What are the actions of friendship? What is it you do when you are being a friend? What are the most important actions in being a friend? What would you look for in the actions of others to determine their friendship?

9. **WORDS.** Now let's turn to the more traditional way of establishing meaning: your thoughts and words. How would you define friendship in your own terms? What are some other words with the same meaning? Can you think of short sayings or mottoes that give meaning to friendship? Try to capture your personal meaning of friendship through your own words, or words from books and movies. Are

there books, or other media, that you associate with friendship?

10. **TIME.** Does friendship have a special time? Is there a time of day, part of the week, a season of the year that you associate with friendship? Is there a time in your life — a time in the past when friendship was especially important? What about its tempo — does friendship have a special rhythm, a cadence, a beat? Can you dance to its rhythm?

11. **PLACE.** What about its place? Does friendship have a special place in your home, your neighborhood, your community? Is there a location in the world that you associate especially with friendship? Is there a special place in the world you associate with being a friend?

12. **PEOPLE.** Finally, consider people who represent your meaning of friendship — people who are good examples of being a friend. Think about people in your family, those you have only read about, people real or imagined who are somehow associated with friendship. Jot down what comes to mind.

Action

Looking over the two or three most important meanings you've noted, and select one
to use as your action guide for the next few
days. It may be a thought, feeling, sound,
or something else, but try to use it to guide
your actions during the next few days. If
your association is the softness of a touch, for
example, keep this in mind throughout the
day to guide your actions toward welcoming
the Spirit of Friendship.

FINDING YOUR PERSONAL IMAGE GUIDE

Look over your meaning map to select another of
the meanings that seems important; it will become
your image guide. You might select a sound, such as a
melody that represents friendship for you: "If I were
this melody…" Or you might select a person: "If I
were the Dalai Lama …" Your image might come
from something you have read: "If I were this poem
…" Select one of your meanings, which you can then
imagine by saying to yourself: "If I were a …"

FINAL ACTION

Before applying your image guide to your daily life,
spend some time practising becoming your image

when you are alone. After you have practised following your image guide a few times, try it out with a companion. Be patient and pay close attention to what happens.

Once you have learned the value of your chosen guide, you may want to return to your meaning map and select another image guide to follow.

MY IMAGE OF FRIENDSHIP: THE GOSSAMER TRAMPOLINE

I imagine I am bouncing on a very special trampoline whose base is woven by gossamer strands of friendship, delicate as rose petals yet strong as steel. The strands of friendship are connected to all my family members and friends, who encircle and support the trampoline. I feel connected to each strand through the surge of energy coming from their loving support. It is energy that is fuelled by friendship and love. I am grateful for this mysterious energy, and offer my support in return. Each of us has own special trampoline, and I am glad to support my family and friends in return.

Part Three:

How I Am Learning to Be a Friend

I cannot recall any other experience with more personal value or surprises than learning to be a friend. My motivation for developing a personal guide was to increase the flow of friendship in my life, and it has more than fulfilled this purpose. Even more important, I have discovered that I am not only learning to be a friend, I am learning to live my life by being true to myself. In this final part of the book I will describe how I am learning to be a friend to highlight its enormous personal value. I will give you an example of how you too can enjoy these benefits by identifying and following your own guide to friendship. I offer my experience only as an example of *how* to develop your own guide, not to tell you *what* to believe. Nothing is more important in learning to be a friend than discovering your own distinct beliefs about friendship and expressing them in your own terms. My experience is exciting, satisfying, and often challenging, but always more than worth the effort. It is a precious opportunity to discover my true beliefs and it is only through being true to our beliefs that we can learn to be true to ourselves. My message is simple: as we learn to be a friend, we learn to be true to ourselves.

I. My Personal Guide to Friendship

It was only recently that I realized the value of personally meaningful action guides to learning to be a friend. I used to focus only on identifying my beliefs in abstract terms, sometimes as ideal qualities, such as openness, or in general mottoes, such as the Golden Rule or the Serenity Prayer. Bringing out my personal beliefs was an important first step, but I gradually realized that putting my beliefs into practice required an equally important next step: translating my beliefs into practical, relevant action guides. I discovered the necessity of this step in my workshop exercises when I tried to act on my beliefs. For example, in Exercise 8, Making Space for the Others, my specific action guide was to imagine that I was a host who wanted to welcome someone into my home. Following this specific action guide helped me accomplish the abstract goal of making space. I developed several specific action guides in these workshop exercises, which further convinced me of their value and led to the development of the guides I describe in this section.

In Part One I described how the emergence of Letting Go, Opening Up, and Accepting became the basic beliefs for my workshops as well as for my personal life. However, when I tried to apply these, I often found that they were too abstract to guide my actions. So, my next step was to turn them into practical terms — to make them my own in my private language — in order to apply them in my daily life. It took some time, but I gradually developed three personal guides expressed in my own language, which actually worked.

To "let go" became "Lighten Up … and Smile." In a similar way, "to open up" became "Stay Open Under Duress" and "to accept" became "Accept … That's All." Following these specific guides was helpful only when my actions were infused by my belief in the Spirit of Friendship, which I translated as "Honour the Mystery." I was pleased that my action guides seemed to be both compact and comprehensive:

To Let Go	Lighten Up … and Smile
To Open Up	Stay Open Under Duress
To Accept	Accept … That's All
To Honour the Mystery	Honour the Spirit of Friendship

This table is simply for the sake of communication. Although it may make the action guides look as though they simply appeared to me, the transition from my purpose to personal action guides took time, effort, and patience. Despite the challenges, I want to you to know the enormous personal value of finding and following your own personal action guides. When I initially began to follow my action guides, I was glad to observe their effect on increasing the flow of friendship, but I also discovered that the more I practised these guides, the more valuable they became. I originally tried to "Lighten Up ... and Smile" because I thought that using humour was a good thing, and while this is still true, lightening up was much more than that. As I learned to lighten up, I was delighted to find that it made me feel alive. In addition to encouraging the flow of friendship, lightening up opened my life force.

In the case of "Staying Open Under Duress," my initial belief was that it meant to simply be open and be receptive. Practising this guide revealed that it required more than being passively receptive. Following the suggestions of master jazz pianist Keith Jarrett, I learned that staying open under duress called for me to let in my experience, recognize it, and allow it reveal itself. As I became more actively open, it became much more valuable and revealed new possibilities.

My following my guide to "Accept...That's All" also turned out to be more than to passively receive. In this case, the more I practised accepting in this way, the more I realized that it involved my active appreciation of the other person or situation. It offered another example of the surprising consequences of being true to myself. When I genuinely accept the other person or situation, it can lead to an awareness of some of their unsuspected features: acceptance leads to appreciation and revelation.

My final guide, "Honour the Mystery," is essential for applying each of the three action guides. In each case, when I try to follow one of my actions I need to imbue it with an underlying acknowledgment of the power of the Spirit of Friendship. Honouring the mystery is the most important guide and the most difficult to communicate, but I will try — as I will with all the guides — in the sections that follow.

LIGHTEN UP ... AND SMILE

Much to my surprise, the familiar cliché, "lighten up," turned out to be a very helpful action guide as I learned to be a friend. I usually thought of it as a shorthand message to someone else to stop being so serious.

Like most important developments in my life, my learning to lighten up was slow, unpredictable, sometimes illogical, and always surprising.

How It Developed

Opening up has been one of my basic beliefs for a long time, but I also discovered along the way the necessity of letting go of obstacles in order to be open. That is why I emphasize learning to let go in my workshops. In my efforts to let go, I imagined I possessed an invisible inner system similar to the circulatory system of blood vessels that flowed through my body. My imaginary system allows the life force to flow, just as the blood flows through my arteries. And just as a clot could block the flow of blood, the flow in my life force could be blocked by an obstacle, such as a persistent fear. Early on, I became aware of the problems created by my dominant mind machine, which often blocked the connection to my feelings and emotions. I was keenly aware that my overly controlling mind was like a clot, but my efforts to deal with this imaginary blockage were not very successful. I came to agree with Benjamin Shields who wrote, "Letting go is one of the most difficult challenges human beings ever face."

Along with the "Letting Go" poem, I also found that a guided imagery exercise to identify an individual's personal image of fun and humour has been very helpful. When I tried this exercise, my image of fun and humour turned out to be a clown playing a saxophone! Identifying my own image of humour was valuable, but more important was the feeling that came from my connecting to my inner sense of fun. I felt light, relieved, and joyful. I noticed that most workshop participants also found this connection enjoyable, and surprisingly helpful. Without initially being aware of its enormous potential value, I began to connect with my inner sense of fun to deal with difficult situations.

When I began to use this new action guide, I considered its positive effects. I imagined that my lightening up renewed the flow of my life force and friendship through shifting my attention. It did not completely remove the obstacle, but my new light-heartedness did diminished the size of the obstacle. Somehow, the obstacle appeared less formidable and no longer controlled all of my experience. Lightening up even helped me deal with my dominating mind machine. When I lightened up, my relation to my mind machine shifted so that it was no longer dominant and there was room for my life force to flow once more as I reconnected with my feelings.

Imagine my relief to discover that this old cliché about lightening up was the key to "Letting Go" and "Opening Up." The more I practise lightening up, the more valuable it becomes. Yes, it is related to my humour, fun, and playfulness, but it is much more. When I lighten up, I can feel the life force flowing freely as my feelings and outlook improve almost immediately.

It also has a double meaning, so that it not only brings welcome relief from my heavy burdens, but it illuminates my experience so that I see more clearly. This double meaning illustrates a feature of each action guide: they are each connected to both my heart and my head. In this case, to lighten up is heartfelt as it allows the flow of life force to open up and connected to my head as it offers light and clarity to my perceptions and thoughts.

Finally, lightening up is also connected to my body: when I feel the surge of life force and well-being, it ripples up into my lips and I smile. My smile is a genuine signal that I want to be a friend to others and to myself. When I lighten up, there is also an inner smile, as I feel calm and peaceful.

The power of a smile is eloquently captured by the Dalai Lama:

> For me, human beings' ability to smile is one of our most beautiful characteristics.... Even in the case of someone I have nothing to do with, when this person smiles at me, I am touched. But why? The answer surely is that a genuine smile touches something fundamental in us: our natural appreciation of kindness.

Even in the middle of the city, strangers sometimes smile at one another. The Dalai Lama emphasizes how one person's smile represents kindness. I find that when my smile is returned, this exchange of kindness is the beginning of a connection, even the possibility of a friendship. If breathing is the essence of the personal, then smiling is the essence of the interpersonal.

Sometimes I begin with a smile and sometimes the smile emanates from my lightening up. I try to honour the essence of whimsy by not analyzing this too much. My favorite way to lighten up is to listen to Sam Pilafin play "When You're Smilin'" on his tuba. His huffing and puffing through this golden-oldie is somehow the epitome of lightening up.

Learning to Lighten Up

None of my guides to friendship is more valuable than lightening up, but learning to follow it is not easy. Like all my earlier experiences in trying new approaches, learning to lighten up is time-consuming and contradictory: it is more than simply connecting with my sense of humour. It means learning to be light in my heart with my feelings, in my body as I move and in my perceptions as I look and listen with a gentle lightness. It takes time because it must permeate all my being.

Lightening up may also result in delight or occasional disappointment. For example, I may choose the wrong time to focus on the silliness of a situation or another person. Lightening up does not lend itself to logical analysis, yet I find that trying to follow it is worthwhile even though it is often neither predictable nor understandable. Choosing to lighten up is a good thing! I feel more alive when I lighten up no matter how it turns out. As I lighten up, I also honour the mystery of the Spirit of Friendship.

I originally tried to lighten up by using logic to connect with my sense of humour; I took a serious approach to becoming light. How foolish could I be! Somehow, I came to my senses and laughed at myself and, even more to the point, I realized that opening to foolishness — my own and all of it in the world — is a surprisingly valuable way to lighten up. It is almost impossible to stay in a heavy, serious mood when I shift my attention to reflect on the foolishness of my taking myself too seriously. Its immediate effect is to puncture the heavy shell, relieving burdens, if only temporarily. Its more lasting result is to reconnect me with my humanity. To be foolish is to be human and to acknowledge my foolishness is to know that I am human. And it was through living my image, of the clown with the saxophone, by playing a saxophone myself, that I learned the enormous value of opening to foolishness in order to lighten up.

The jazz band I play in is called The Foolish Things, after a 1930s ballad by that name. Playing alto sax in our band is one of my favorite ways to lighten up and have fun. We are The Foolish Things and we try to live by our name. We have lots of fun, never criticize anyone's playing, and keep our day jobs! Every Friday at a nearby pub, we play the music of Gershwin, Cole Porter, Kern, Ellington, Rodgers and Hart, and Hoagie Carmichael; timeless tunes we know by heart. Being a Foolish Thing, I don't worry if I hit a wrong note ... maybe I am onto some new variation. Maybe being in The Foolish Things means I can really be myself. I certainly feel a difference with less pressure and more freedom.

This is not a lack of responsibility or direction, quite the opposite. By playing with The Foolish Things, I get clarity so that when I am playing a tune like "All the Things You Are" all of my attention is focused on the music and I can really hear it. I have no musical background, so I know nothing about the theory and chord structure of this piece. My appreciation of the beauty in Jerome Kern's classic ballad comes entirely from my taking it in and trying to express it. And as the music flows, I can also feel the flow of friendship as we play together.

Being a musical Foolish Thing is great, but it does not mean that I lighten up all the time, or that it always yields all of its benefits. There is time to be whimsical and a time to be serious. It is always a question of whether it is a time to focus on foolishness or on being serious. It is not always easy to lighten up when I'm experiencing pressure from external forces or from inner heavy feelings. I try to accept my heavy mood in the same way I might try to accept my friends' sadness, without judging, simply taking it in. Sometimes staying open to accept my dark mood relieves the heaviness enough that I can lighten up. At other times I need to shift my attention from accepting the heaviness to becoming aware of how foolish it would be to continue to wallowing in the dark mood. I am not always able to lighten up immediately, but it always makes me feel better when I can. It also helps me feel more confident so that I can focus my attention on my intended actions.

STAY OPEN UNDER DURESS

I have emphasized the importance of staying open to ourselves and our experience in all my professional efforts to encourage personal development, as well as in my personal attempts to open up in my daily life. Openness occupied a central role in my writing. *Beginning with Ourselves* discussed opening up to yourself, while *The Renewal of Personal Energy* featured learning to permit the inner flow of energy necessary for renewal and combating burnout. On the personal side of things, when I followed my own advice to stay open, I felt more alive and in touch with myself and my surroundings. Unfortunately, I was not always able to stay open. I realize now that too often when I experienced difficulty from within or without, I closed down. If my mood took a turn to the dark side or had an interpersonal disagreement, I would cut myself off from my feelings and either go on autopilot or seek a distraction. This cut me off from myself and what was happening around me. It also closed the flow of my life force and the flow of friendship.

Of course, there are times when it is necessary to close down for self-protection, but I realized that there are many times when staying open while experiencing difficulty may be the best action of choice. Whether the need to close down comes from personal discomfort or interpersonal conflict, I have gradually discovered the surprising value of exerting the extra effort to stay open. Thomas Moore expressed this value eloquently:

> Especially in moments of conflict and maybe even despair, being open to the demands of a relationship can provide an extraordinary opportunity for self-knowledge. It provides an

occasion to glimpse your own soul and notice its longings and fears. And as you get to know yourself, you can become more accepting and understanding of the other's depth of soul.

My personal action guide for being open in such circumstances is, "Stay Open Under Duress." Following this action guide is my personal antidote to automatically closing down at the first signs of difficulty. I do not follow this in every situation, but this guide reminds me that I always have a choice.

How It Developed

My experience in the Ornish Open Your Heart support group was my wake-up call to the special importance of staying open under duress. I have already described how Dean Ornish's message of openness as survival took on personal meaning through my living his suggestions by opening to myself and others in our support group.

Staying Open as Survival

Through Dean Ornish's Open Your Heart support group, I learned the importance of staying open under duress as a means of survival. As cardiac survivors, we knew the importance of learning to open our hearts under all conditions. We tried to follow Ornish's suggestion:

When we are able to open our hearts at all levels — anatomically, emotionally, and spiritually — we can live every moment in fullness.

The first thing I learned when I tried to follow Ornish's advice was the importance of first letting go, or lightening up. Earlier, I described the practical value of learning to lighten up and open up through my weekly support group experience, but an even more important benefit came from trying to open my heart in my daily life between our Tuesday night sessions. Through many attempts to open my heart I began to learn the language of the heart.

Learning the Language of the Heart

As I learned to open up to my own and other's feelings, I imagined that I was also learning to appreciate friendship in a new language: the language of my heart. I imagined that when I described a situation in which I was feeling happy or sad that I was doing so in two distinct languages — the language of the situation and the language of the heart, or how I felt as it happened. I then saw myself trying to learn to speak from my heart and listen from my heart.

The language of the heart is rendered in many ways. Sometimes through words: *heartfelt, heartsick, light of heart, heavy of heart, from the bottom of my heart.* Sometimes through images: I was flying high, I felt like a rat in the corner. The language of the heart is also revealed by non-verbal cues, such as tone of voice and body language. Knowing this, I could focus on learning the language and using it to open myself to the flow of friendship, which travelled according with the language of the heart.

As I listened to one of my group members, I tried to focus all of my attention on how he or she was feeling and, of course, I used my own emotions as the antenna for sensing theirs. Learning the language of the heart also helped me respond after I had listened and tried to sense my friend's expression of feelings. Because the language of the heart is often non-verbal, I learned to accept the value of nodding my head as a signal that I had listened from my heart. As I tried to respond to the other person with empathy, my thoughts flashed back to my experience as a psychotherapist and I recalled the expression, "Listening with the third ear." It was by no means my first effort to connect with my feelings and the feelings of others, rather a continuing effort to learn to be open to the flow of friendship.

Staying Open as Revelation

My love of music helped me appreciate the value of openness, especially staying open when I was tempted to close down. Just as I learned to lighten up through making music with The Foolish Things, I also learned the value of staying open through the words and music of master jazz pianist Keith Jarrett. Jarrett is not only one of the finest jazz pianists in the world, but also a talented writer. I was profoundly moved by the following description of his "rendez-vous with music," because his words apply exactly to my attempt for a "rendezvous with friendship." I read it often and it always offers excitement and insight so I hope you will share my enthusiasm as you read it for the first time:

> A master jazz musician goes onto the stage hoping to have a rendezvous with music. He/she knows the music is there (it always is), but this meeting depends not only on knowledge, but on openness. It must be let in, recognized, and revealed to the listener, the first of whom is the musician him/herself. This recognition is the most misunderstood part of the process (even by musicians). It is a discrimination against mechanical pat-tern, for content, against habit, for surprise, against easy virtuosity, for saying more with less, against facile emotion, for a certain quality of energy, against stasis, for flow, against military precision, for tactile pulse. It is like an attempt, over and over again, to reveal the heart of things.

His succinct definition of openness as being "let in, recognized, and revealed" is profound and universally applicable. When I substitute the word *friendship* for *music*, his words capture the purpose of my book —"a rendezvous with friendship" — as well as the purpose of each chapter — to let friendship in, recognize it, and allow it to reveal itself. I realize Jarrett has captured my purpose more clearly than I ever could.

When I attended one of Jarrett's concerts, his credo was on display the whole time. He moved vigorously and occasionally stood in embodied recognition of the music. He also occasionally uttered sounds of delight as he discovered a new revelation in the music. Living his credo of openness created a "rendezvous with music," which was especially evident in his heartfelt rendition of his signature tune, "When I Fall in Love." It was music of the moment, never before and never again, but revealed for now with breathtaking beauty.

"To be let in, recognized, and revealed." I am amazed at how this expression of openness applies to so many other aspects of life besides music. Because of their universal applicability, I will use these words as the basis of my description of my various experiences of opening up. My understanding of these three features —to be let in, recognized, and revealed — is that they represent a spirit of openness rather than a methodical sequence of steps. When I try to apply Jarrett's suggestion in my "rendezvous with friendship," I often find that once they are let in, the recognition and revelation occur simultaneously.

Jarrett is also eloquent on the meaning of the heart:

We can say our heart is beating in order for us to have our next meal, or in order to find our real purpose in life. The fact is, however, that we can say nothing if our heart isn't beating, and it's as far from a drum machine as anything can be.

Opening to the New Day: What Does the Day Say?

I want to open myself to the new day, to take in its meaning and possibilities. Every day is special, and I greet each day, whether it is sunny or snowing, Monday or Friday. I stay open under duress, for example, by going out on a snowy, cold Monday in February to connect with this particular day, which will not come again. My habit of greeting the new day is inspired both by Ornish, "To live every moment in fullness," and Jarrett, the day needs to be "let in, recognized, and revealed."

Here is how I greet the new day. First thing in the morning, I go out on the balcony, sit down, and focus on my breathing. Then I focus my attention on the question, "What does the day say?" I try to synchronize with this special day, to feel its rhythm and to get in touch with it. I try to recognize the day not only through my eyes and ears, but through my nose, taste buds, and skin. I sit quietly and patiently waiting for the day to reveal itself. The answer may come in what I see, the clouds, or what I hear, the song of the dove. It may come in what I smell, a fragrant aroma from a lilac tree, or what I feel on my skin, a gentle breeze.

In Jarrett's terms, I try to recognize this day and allow it to reveal its message in a few words. I carry this revelation with me to guide my actions throughout the day. I try to recognize the message as fully as possible through my feelings and my body so that I can apply it in my actions. Here is an example: The clouds move slowly and quietly in an unhurried procession. The message for this day: "Move gently." I try to carry this message into my actions of the day by focusing on my breath. This is to remind me to move gently, not only in my actions, but in my feelings, senses, and thoughts. The sun peeks up over the horizon, shyly finding its path for the day. The message is that of the old song, "Softly, as in a morning sunrise."

I might rely also on my breathing as my signal, since each new inhalation brings a fresh supply of air. In this case I may need a special effort to overcome my old habits of taking things for granted. But today is fresh. Sometimes it seems the day does not respond to my question, but often when I stay open to the answer, I find the day is revealing the message of "Silence."

Honouring silence has been one of the most rewarding messages I have experienced because doing so often reveals a surprise. This morning, the answer was: "Be calm." I plant my feet firmly on the ground to let myself know that I am anchored and that is safe for me to remain calm.

These are some examples of two ways I greet the day and trying to honour its message. There are also days when the message is less than clear, as well as days when I have difficulty keeping the message in mind. I am never able to apply the message all day, but I find that making the effort to synchronize myself with the day makes me feel better. In addition to posing this question, I also focus on opening to *today* for its special possibilities.

Learning to Stay Open Under Duress

I have no doubt that staying open under duress is a very helpful guide to follow in being a friend, but knowing its value in words is no guarantee I can apply it to my actions in everyday life. No matter how compelling its logic, staying open under duress is an action guide whose value depends on how well I apply it. That is why writing this book involves both words and action. Each day after I finish writing about an action guide, I try to learn more about its action value by applying it to my day. I try to live what I have written, using my daily experience as a living laboratory. In the past, when I experienced disagreement with a friend, for example, I found that staying open under duress helped to sustain my friendship ties. In other situations, even when I have been unable to remain open, keeping it in mind helps me live my life smoothly.

As I try to practise staying open under duress, I am keenly aware of my frequent failures to follow my guide. My experience is a living example of what it is like to try to follow this action guide: I feel like a batter in a baseball game, knowing I have to keep swinging even though I will fail more often than I succeed. I am able to open up enough to accept that I cannot always follow this guide, and the acceptance of my failures as well as my success in following this guide helps me appreciate the true meaning of "Staying Open Under Duress."

Changing my lifelong habit of closing down at the first signs of difficulty is a challenge. My initial motivation was curiosity about what might happen if I stayed open, and when I discovered that it often revealed new possibilities, my desire grew stronger. Learning to stay open under duress has not been as big a test of my strength of character as one might imagine, but following this guide helps me come alive and become more closely connected with myself and my experience.

In practice, staying open is an active, alive awareness that is keenly attentive to what is happening. This active focusing of attention helps you better understand and accept you current experience, which often allows you to gain a better understanding of the difficulty you might be experiencing. And these benefits will increase your desire to continue to try to follow this guide, which helps make it achievable.

Staying open under duress has gradually become something I can readily choose to do. I don't always choose it because there are times when I need to close down for self-protection. There are also many times when I try to stay open, but am unable to do so. I find that my attempts to follow this guide are similar to my earlier attempts to lighten up, in that the more I learn to practise staying open under duress, the more it blends into the other two guides of lightening up and accepting, and the more it becomes an avenue to help me come alive.

I have described examples of staying open to internal difficulty, such as fatigue or a dark and heavy mood. But there are even greater challenges that come from outside, things such as interpersonal conflict or disagreement. Staying open under duress during an interpersonal disagreement is more challenging because it can be difficult to remain open when in the midst of a heated argument. This happened recently and I was able to stay open, which was very helpful. When I took a moment to ensure that I was being open, I stopped talking. I could see myself and the other person in a more detached, calm way and this new perspective helped me to transcend to a different view of what was happening. With a glimpse of lightheartedness at my role in the situation, I was able to let my ego go a little. Staying open did not solve the disagreement completely, but it made me see it in a new light.

Staying open under duress definitely does not mean that I am trying to eliminate the duress, indeed quite the opposite. If I stay open to feeling disappointed, for example, it means that I accept my feelings of disappointment for what they are, while also realizing they will not last forever. It does not eliminate my negative feelings, but they slowly diminish in size so that they no longer engulf me. It is as if my feelings are like another person whom I have accepted and they respond with appreciation. It is important to emphasize that timing is everything in staying open under duress. I must choose when and how to stay open; I have no recipe for these choices. What is important is that I have the capability of remaining opening under duress when I choose to do so.

ACCEPT ... THAT'S ALL

Acceptance is the essence of friendship and my following the special meaning of this action guide, "Accept... That's All," is at the heart of being a friend. Learning to accept means taking in whatever I am experiencing, whether it be an idea, another person, my personal difficulties, or my life. I do not choose to take in each and every experience, but they are always present as possibilities for living my life fully. In addition to its being a general credo, acceptance also has a special personal meaning in relation to being a friend. For instance, when I offer my friendship through my actions.

I was surprised to discover that often I could best express my acceptance by doing and saying nothing, just being with my friend ... that's all. I want my active acceptance to clearly reflect only my friendly intentions, nothing more, and the additional phrase, "that's all" helps me do so.

This action guide is closely related to the other two, in that all three are aimed at helping my acceptance. When I lighten up, I accept myself and when I open up, it often initiates my acceptance of myself and others. I have finally realized that these three action guides are very similar in their reminding me that to be a friend is to accept attentively and to do so is imbued with the Spirit of Friendship.

How It Developed

Carl Rogers' principle of unconditional acceptance springs to mind when I try to identify the early beginnings of my experience with acceptance. I first knew its importance in my experience as a psychotherapist and later realized its importance for friendship. As often happens, I knew its value in words, but often found it difficult to apply in my actions. Put simply, the phrase, "unconditional acceptance" was too abstract. I needed to translate unconditional acceptance into my own personal language to direct my actions. "Accept...That's All" gradually emerged as my personal shorthand for practising unconditional acceptance.

First, I felt that the phrase unconditional acceptance seemed to emphasize what it was not, rather than what it was. I wanted to focus all of my attention on my positive intentions of offering my friendship, nothing more. To do so, I imbued my actions with my belief in the Spirit of Friendship. I was interested in identifying the variety of actions for offering my friendship — greeting, listening, helping, and gift giving — but whatever my actions, what mattered most was my genuine desire to offer my friendship.

Second, I needed a personal reminder to keep my actions pure and simple, reflecting only my desire to express my friendship, nothing more. This is where "that's all" came in. "That's all" is associated in my mind with the lyrics of a old ballad by the same name, but how it became associated with my acceptance of friendship is not as obvious: it came about gradually in ways that are not easy to capture. I think the first time I was aware of its action value was in relation to my gift giving. I wanted my giving a gift to another person to be a pure action of my friendship, nothing more. Yet I realized that my actions often reflected many implicit expectations. Would the person thank me? Would the person reciprocate? Would the person appreciate my friendly gesture? All of these ego-based expectations diminished my intended purpose of expressing my friendship. In this case, "that's all" meant letting my ego go by setting aside my expectations for self-benefit in order to purify my act of friendship.

Letting my ego go when I offer a gift can be especially difficult: on the one hand, I want to disregard the effect of my giving a gift, on the other hand, I am always pleased when the other reciprocates or expresses gratitude. As much as I may hope that my friend will actively respond to my friendly action, I cannot control their response and the more I attempt to do so, the less it will lead to friendly relations. When I receive a gift, I can usually sense the intent of the gift giver. Some gifts are duty gifts, with almost no personal meaning; some gifts seem intended to evoke a response, either a gift in return or expressing my thanks. Occasionally there are gifts that come with no strings attached, given simply as a token of friendship. I usually feel free, in these instances, and often return the favour, which strengthens the friendship tie.

I also came to appreciate the value of "Accept... that's all" in relation to greeting and responding to others greeting me. I consider greeting other people with "good morning" to be the simplest way to express my acceptance of them, as well as my friendship, nothing more. I do not concern myself with whether the person responds or not. Oddly enough, my poor vision helped me realize there may be many reasons why a person might not respond, which have nothing to do with me. I often cannot recognize people who know me, for instance, until they are very close and they might interpret my not responding as a social snub. My practise of "that's all" is my way of accepting that I cannot know why or how the other person will respond, so I can let it go without judging or misinterpreting. In this case, "that's all" helps me accept our differences, as well as the fact that I cannot know everything. I greet them ... that's all.

The more my gesture of acceptance is free of control, the more my friend is free to choose how to respond. This is true when someone greets me, just as when I receive a gift, and I can often sense the pure intention of friendship. The back-and-forth of friendship comes from our genuine desire for friendship, not from any form of control.

No matter how I express my acceptance, "that's all," as a reminder to let go of control, also has special meanings for different actions. When I focus on myself so that I can accept my mistakes, "that's all" means focusing on the future rather than wallowing in the past. When I focus on accepting another person, it means to temporarily set aside the person's differences from myself and my beliefs. When I focus on our friendship ties, it means emphasizing our relationship by setting aside my personal challenges. It also means, "We are still friends."

Finally, I realized that my understanding of "that's all" was also my version of the "Serenity Prayer":

Give me the Serenity to accept the things

I cannot change,

The Courage to change the things I can, and

The Wisdom to know the difference.

LEARNING TO ACCEPT … THAT'S ALL

I have been trying to accept myself and others for many years, even though I only recently became aware of the importance of including "that's all." I want to offer examples of my experiences, with the repeated reminder that such acceptance is an ideal that I am not always able to follow.

Accepting Myself

My personal experience with self-acceptance is drawn from the two workshop exercises on accepting my capabilities, my foolishness, and limitations. My vision loss will serve as a good example of how I tried to accept one of my limitations.

Accepting My Vision Loss

I have always had poor vision, although in the early days, wearing glasses brought my near-sighted 20/600 eyes pretty close to 20/20. When I enlisted in the army for the Second World War, they thought the correction was good enough to make me a machine gunner. However, when we went into the battle line in Patton's Third Army, the other members of my squad insisted that I carry a spare pair of glasses!

About twenty years ago, my vision took a turn for the worse and I found myself unable to read without some powerful means of magnification. I frantically tried magnifying lamps and increasingly thick glasses lenses before I discovered the monocular lens, which helped me to read. My visual limitation also affected my teaching methods, not to mention other professional and personal activities. I was well-aware of losing my vision, but it took some time to learn to accept it and to change my actions.

The easy solution would have been to take early retirement, but my teaching was much too important to give up. I never considered it an option.

Rather, I gradually accepted my limitation through developing new ways of teaching and relied even more on group discussion and interaction with my students. I tried to accept my limitation … that's all, no regrets, no self-pity. As I began to accept my vision loss, I became less certain that others would accept it. In faculty meetings, I was keenly aware of how others would react when I brought out my monocular. My initial fears faded, though, as I discovered that if I accepted myself, others were likely to accept me as well.

I did not learn to accept myself and my visual limitation entirely on my own. My wife was consistently supportive without making me dependent on her, allowing me to discover what I could and could not do. I was also very fortunate to find a low-vision support group, which was very helpful in many ways. The group helped me to accept my own handicap. Although I am focusing on self-acceptance here, it is impossible to completely separate accepting myself from accepting others and their acceptance of me. This experience was a reminder of the distinctive value of support groups as they allow kindred spirits to come together for both friendly acceptance and first-hand knowledge about our limitations. Later, as I have described, my Open Your Heart support was equally helpful. After joining it, I drew up a cartoon to show my wife, in which a little man was saying, "I hope nothing else happens to me. I don't have time for any more support groups."

When I accept myself as completely as possible, I feel less threatened. I am not as concerned with comparing myself with others, either through competition or possible loss of my ability. To accept myself ... that's all is an ideal guide, which I occasionally find difficult to follow. But I know its value from those times when I am able to do so. When I follow it, I not only feel better about myself, but it also helps me accept others with less concern about how they will respond. I learn once more the simple truth that to accept another, I need to accept myself.

How Am I Like and Different from Others?

When I translate the three principles about persons being like and different to myself, it becomes:

1. How am I like every other person?
2. How am I like some other people?
3. How am I like no other person?

These general questions are the foundation for becoming aware of and accepting myself: the more I am able to understand the first question, the better able I will be to accept others. This is also true of the other two questions since I realize that, just as I am like some others and distinct from all others, so it is with the other person I hope to accept. Workshop participants have also found that considering these questions helped reveal their own humanity and kindred spirits.

Accepting Others

As I discussed in the workshop exercises, listening attentively is one of the most important actions for being a friend.

Listening and Letting My Ego Go

Following my guide to "Accept ... That's All" means that I must focus all of my attention on listening to the other person. To do so I need to let my ego go and make mental space for taking the person in. It means to "Listen... That's All." I not only try to make space for the other person as in Exercise 8, but I also take the time to listen. Offering space and time are genuine signals of friendship.

I realize the importance of taking the time to listen when I recall my own experiences of being cut-off by someone who "did not have time for me." In the time pressured world of 24/7, we have created the euphemism "quality time" to describe the importance of taking time out for others. Quality time is often used to describe a remote luxury, rather than an experience that we can have often. I can choose to offer my time to another person: it is usually a welcome and tangible sign of my being a friend.

Attentive listening means not only offering time and space, but it also calls for recording my impressions in memory. Friendship ties are gradually woven in large part as we recall our earlier meetings, and nothing is more telling as a signal of friendship than to be remembered.

I also like to remind myself that I do not have to respond to everything someone says or does. I often remember my mother's simple response to someone's description of personal trouble or difficulty: a drawn-out "Welllllll ..." followed by a smile. That's all. She did not have to respond verbally to each and every statement. I like to emulate her response, with my version: "Listen *and* Accept... That's All."

Accepting Others Who Are Similar and Different

When I am with a friend, I don't only focus on our similarities, but I try to be open and accepting to our differences. On those occasions when I am able to properly communicate my acceptance of our differences, I find that it leads to a stronger friendship bond. It is another example of the magical effects of "Accept... That's All." I need to overcome a lifetime of focusing only on agreement and similarity in order to shift my focus and listen for differences and distinctions, and doing so means that I am more likely to learn about my friend's heart's desires. Becoming aware of differences allows me to encourage my friend's personal development.

When I am with someone I don't get along with, my approach is exactly the opposite. I try to focus my attention on our similarities and play down our differences in order to accept the person. This practice can be very difficult. But I try to apply my action guides to every situation so that I can attempt to accept everyone ... that is all.

All of these approaches also apply when I try to strengthen my friendship ties with family members or close friends. I need to listen carefully to appreciate their present concerns and feelings, so that I am aware of any changes in their circumstances. I need to remind myself that this is important, because the better I know someone, the more likely I am to take them for granted and not listen attentively. Only through continual attention to my family member's current state can I accept them to strengthen our tie of friendship. This may often require my changing myself, which is the key to sustaining and strengthening our friendship tie.

HONOUR THE MYSTERY

In Part One I described how the ideas of Thomas Moore and John O'Donohue helped develop my understanding of "Honouring the Mystery." In this section, I will describe how this understanding imbues my actions with the Spirit of Friendship. Following my action guides is one step in being a friend, but unless my actions are imbued with the Spirit of Friendship, they are unlikely to encourage the flow of friendship in my life. "Honouring the Mystery" is my personal guide for infusing the Spirit of Friendship into my actions. When I honour the mystery, I take on a special way of being, which strongly influences my actions. Although quite different from my other action guides, "Honouring the Mystery" complements my actions by accentuating their friendly nature and calls for me to give up control.

To honour the mystery is a paradox. It means that friendship is more likely to flow when I stop trying to control it and let it happen. Given my logical nature, it is not easy to give up my desire to know everything about friendship so that I can control it. I try to deal with this paradox with a combination of approaches. On the one hand, I continue to try to follow my action guides to Letting Go, Open Up, and Accept, while on the other hand, I accept the essential role of the Spirit of Friendship by acknowledging that I cannot control the flow of friendship. I honour its mysterious spirit — which is quite different from following action guides.

My personal experience in trying of honouring the mystery is itself quite mysterious and hard to describe. I can best describe my experience by saying that I called on specific qualities within to help myself honour it properly. These inner qualities offer a means for me to access a way of being how I want to be. So when I focus on a quality such as patience, it saturates all of my experience as I see and hear patiently, feel patiently, act patiently, think patiently. I realize this sounds unrealistic; of course, even though I focus on a quality, it does not mean I will always be able to apply it in all that I feel, perceive, do, and think. But it provides a focus, which opens the possibility for numerous actions.

I will describe three qualities that help me honour the mystery: trust, patience, and curiosity. Remember that these are qualities that have personal value for me and I do not expect them to have similar meaning and value for you.

TRUST

Trust is my article of faith in friendship; it allows me to honour its mystery. My trust in friendship helps me realize that it is not always necessary to know everything, indeed that I need to accept my ignorance. To admit that I do not, and cannot, know everything about friendship is a simple and essential step in letting go of control and honouring the mystery. I am able to relinquish control, in large part, because of my awareness of the continuous presence of friendship within me. I have learned to trust that friendship is always there, within me and within others, if it is allowed to flourish. I also realize that my trusting myself to be a friend will not guarantee that others will respond in kind, but I continue to trust the Spirit.

To Honour the Mystery Is like to "Accept ... That's All"

In this case I accept the paradox that I know some things and but not others ... that's all. Once I have broken through the barriers and admitted that I don't know everything about friendship, my admission not only brings relief, but may also help bring new insights.

My basic trust in the Spirit of Friendship is similar to my faith in the trust that underlies my friendship ties. I described this trust in the exercise on "appreciating your friendship tie as it is today." Honouring the Mystery depends on the same kind of underlying trust. Like all of my intentions, I am not always able to trust the Spirit completely, but it remains a basic belief for me and the words, to honour the mystery, and help me sustain my belief.

PATIENCE

For me, patience is the daughter of trust. When I trust the Spirit of Friendship, I am comfortable with my own actions without impatiently waiting for some response. Patience in friendship is based on trusting myself as well as the friendship tie. This trust allows me to accept my friend without needing immediate reassurance. To honour the mystery is to accept … that's all, to simply let it happen.

When I am impatiently preoccupied with worrying about receiving a response from my friend through email, snail mail, or phone, I am cut off from my present experience. When I let go of my preoccupations by trusting patience, I become present to my life.

To Honour the Mystery is to Become Present

Patience provides an active opportunity for completely experiencing my life in the present, rather than experiencing it as an uncomfortably passive endurance of waiting. As I've learned to be patient with friendship, I discover that letting go of my impatient worries actually strengthens friendship ties, as my friend experiences my patience as an acceptance, and even encouragement.

As I described earlier, Rilke advised the young poet to be patient by "living the question." I can best follow Rilke's advice by honouring the mystery and trusting the Spirit. In this case, to be patient is to feel satisfied with following my action guides, knowing that they alone will not suffice, but trusting that I have done my best ... that's all. All of this comes from a fusion of trust and patience, which also focuses more of my attention on my heart, where both Spirit and Mystery dwell.

CURIOSITY

The final ingredient in my recipe for honouring the mystery is the quality of curiosity, which adds spice and energy to my experience. I can focus my curiosity on different friendship features with different intentions and, in this case, my curiosity is focused on what will happen with my friend. My curiosity works in a contradictory way: I am curious to see what will happen when I honour the mystery, yet I do not allow my curiosity to interfere or try to control what may happen.

My curiosity is a lighthearted wonder, bordering on a more serious awe at the miracle of mystery. When I honour the mystery, it is as if I am trying an entirely new experiment to see what will happen and my curiosity has the same intentional itch as I might experience with any experiment.

Whether I am applying one of my three action guides or trying to "Honour the Mystery," living my beliefs calls for some energy and my curiosity is the wellspring of energy for doing so.

II. Friendship Over the Years

My life, like that of most people, is filled with joys and sorrows, hits and misses, as I try to follow my action guides. In this concluding section, I will describe three of my long-time friendships to illustrate my actual experience of learning to be a friend over the years. While the previous section emphasized the value of my ideals, this section is grounded in the reality of trying to follow them. I want to strike a balance to show that while my friendship guides do not make my life perfect, it is very helpful in guiding my actions.

Viewing my earlier experiences of friendship through the lens of my present beliefs led to some interesting discoveries. I found that my earlier actions sometimes showed evidence of my current beliefs, even though I wasn't consciously attempting to follow them. I noticed that some of my friends' actions also seemed to reflect my current beliefs, even though they were not following my specific guides. I also discovered that our friendship was most likely to flow freely when we both lightened up or accepted each other. It was only by recalling my actual experience that I could see the vital importance of our interactions in creating our strong friendship ties.

Here are brief sketches of three of my long-time friendships — more than forty years with my wife, Jan; more than sixty years with my friend, Harry; and more than thirty years with my friends in the

Thursday Group. Even though brief, I hope that my descriptions will show their personal importance for me, as well as the role of my personal guides in strengthening these long-time friendships.

MY FRIENDSHIP WITH MY WIFE, JAN

Nothing is more important to me than my friendship with Jan, my marriage partner and best friend for the past forty-two years. For this book, I decided to view our friendship in terms of my beliefs about being a friend. Specifically, I have considered each of us in terms of lightening up, staying open, and accepting completely.

Jan has a great sense of humour, which often lightens things when I become too serious. My poor-vision clumsiness is often a challenge to her sense of humour, but she usually manages to find a lighthearted means of supporting me. For example, I am of no use at all with things mechanical, and my poor vision doesn't help matters much. Nonetheless, I get intrigued when something— perhaps the TV remote or my tape recorder — doesn't work. Apparently I make a distinctive humming sound when my curiousity about broken objects is piqued: "hmmmm." Jan has learned that this sound is a danger signal: when she hears it, she comes running to snatch whatever mechanical object I have in my hands before I destroy it. And we both laugh! Since I often have more difficulty letting go my serious side, it's such a relief that we can lighten up together.

In contrast, staying open under duress means dealing with conflict, and until recently, I tried to avoid it. Jan thinks that our different reaction to conflict comes partly from our experiences with our siblings. She is the third of four daughters, which gave her many opportunities to learn about conflict and sharing. I, on the other hand, was essentially an only child. My brother is thirteen years younger, so I had little experience with interpersonal conflict growing up. As an adult, I often close down when Jan and I disagree, but talking to her about my resistance to conflict has helped me stay more open, more often.

Here is an example of Jan's openness. When I began playing a saxophone, she gave me a delightful gift: a small, metal figure of a clown playing a saxophone. It was very appropriate, as it symbolized my initial fooling around with the sax, as I learned to play.

Jan's response to my work on this book is a good example of complete acceptance. I have been working on it for several years, but she has never once asked me when I expected to finish. Her wordless support of my writing has been essential to my completing the book. Knowing the value of receiving her support, I wanted to offer her my complete acceptance in return. Unfortunately, I have not always been successful. In the earlier days, I was too often critical without realizing that she had her own reasons for doing things. But I have learned that I do not need to understand all of the reasons for her actions: I need only understand that she has her reasons and accept her ... that's all. I am working on applying this new meaning to my actions. Better late than never!

A few years ago, Jan's life changed dramatically when she was involved in a near fatal accident. She was crossing the street at a crosswalk in front of our apartment building, when she was struck by an SUV. She could have been killed, but fortunately she escaped with serious injuries from which she is still recovering. And as if the accident weren't enough, she suffered a heart attack a few years later. As she continues to recover, she still finds the time to make our home a peaceful haven away from the frantic pace outside our downtown apartment. We enjoy the quiet life of being at home, and no longer do any travelling. But that's ok: give me the simple life.

During the late afternoon, we often sit together before preparing dinner. Sometimes she reads something from the paper to me, sometimes we talk about things that happened to us that day, and at other times we simply sit together and no words are necessary. We have very different lifestyles — Jan is a night owl and I'm a morning glory — so our late afternoon meetings are a good time for us to be together. One afternoon, we were coping with our beta blocker and blood thinner prescriptions when I said, "Honey, we know we are getting older when our pillow talk changes to pill talk!"

One of the most enjoyable things we do together is watch National Football League games. From September to February, we spend most of our Sundays (and Monday evenings) watching NFL football on

TV. Jan gives a new and different meaning to the "Sunday football wife": she is an even more devoted fan than I am. Having grown up in western New York, she is a long-time Buffalo Bills fan, so we agonized through their four Super Bowl losses in the nineties.

Since then, we have kept up our interest in all the teams by creating our own little game where we each try to pick the winners of all the games. Each Sunday at noon, Jan reads the comments and point spread on each game before we each make our selections. Over the years, we are about even, and our little competition increases our enjoyment as we lighten up together. I think it's good for our immune systems.

MY FRIENDSHIP WITH HARRY

Harry and I met in 1949 at Ohio State University, where we were both starting graduate work in clinical psychology. Harry served in the Australian Air Force so we were also both Second World War veterans eager to make up for lost time and get on with our lives. We met in graduate school, but we became close friends later in our first positions as faculty members.

After graduation, we were fortunate to begin our professional careers at two of the top psychology departments in the country; Harry at Princeton and myself at Yale. Each of us quickly discovered that our department maintained its high standing through an intensely competitive climate among junior faculty. Since we weren't too far apart at our new positions — the drive from New Haven to Princeton is only a little over two hours —it wasn't long before we got together again.

When we discussed our new challenges, we decided to do some research together in order to weather the intense pressure to publish. Our decision initiated a close collaboration, which continued for the next fifteen years. In the early days, Harry joined me in New Haven to conduct research on Connecticut schools, while I returned the favor, travelling to Princeton to join Harry in researching New Jersey schools. We collaborated on several research projects, published jointly in refereed journals, and eventually wrote a book together.

I realize in recalling our personal and professional collaboration that we were anticipating Dean Ornish's idea of friendship as survival, since working together helped us survive the perils of the academic publish-or-perish pressure cooker. Our successful professional collaboration was possible in large part because it was based on our close friendship, which exemplified the basic concepts of interdependence and trust. It also mirrored many of my present beliefs about friendship

We continued to work together in the 1960s, but this time with a more practical focus. We were both applied psychologists at heart and the creation of federal programs such as the Peace Corps, Head Start, and Upward Bound gave us wonderful opportunities to apply our theories and research. Even though we were a little further apart due to my relocation to Syracuse in 1959, we continued our close collaboration. For example, Harry headed up a large-scale assessment program for the Peace Corps and I worked on his staff. And when I became director of the National Evaluation of Project Upward Bound, Harry worked with me. It was an exciting and busy time for both of us.

In 1965 my family suffered a terrible shock when my first wife, Pat, died very suddenly and unexpectedly three days before Christmas. Harry and his wife, Chloe, came to the rescue by inviting me and my children to spend Christmas with them over the following two years. I will always be grateful for their gesture of complete acceptance at a time when their friendship meant so much.

In the late 1960s, we each began a new chapter in our lives. In my case, Jan and I got married and moved to Toronto where I could apply my theories and research at the Ontario Institute for Studies in Education. Harry's situation was quite different: his marriage ended and he moved south to Florida to apply his theories to the world of business and management. After fifteen years of very close collaboration, we no longer worked together, but continued to meet on personal visits.

Almost 40 years after meeting at Ohio State, four of us former graduate students — Harry, BJ, Ralph, and I — decided to get together for a reunion. We first met in Tampa in 1987 for a long weekend of fun and friendship, which one of Harry's daughters called "a pajama party for old guys." The reunion was so successful that we continued to hold it each spring for several years, alternating the meeting place from Tampa to LA to Laramie to Toronto.

We continued our reunions until 1994 when Ralph passed away. The following year the three of us resumed the tradition until 1997 when a misunderstanding between Harry and myself ended our reunions — and almost ended our friendship. The difficulty arose when I disagreed with a decision Harry had made. I failed to accept his changing life situation and, as a result, Harry wanted no more reunions. We did not communicate for several months.

I soon realized that I had been out of line: I didn't know all the reasons for his decision, and besides it was none of my business. I saw that my failure to accept … that's all led to our falling out, but it was a little late. Fortunately, the story has a happy ending. After some time passed, Harry accepted my apology and we became friends again, communicating by phone and email. To confirm our re-established friendship, I compiled a description of our work and friendship in a decade-by-decade summary called "Fifty Years of Friendship Between Harry and Dave." It was my way to celebrate for myself and to let Harry know how much our friendship meant.

MY FRIENDSHIP WITH THE THURSDAY GROUP

In addition to its personal importance, the Thursday Group is an interesting case of an informal group that has sustained its vitality for more than thirty years, even though the members in the group have changed over that time. In today's group there are only two of us who were original members.

The story begins in 1976 when I was yearning for an opportunity to share experiences with my colleagues in an informal setting, with no specific agenda. So I invited about a dozen colleagues to meet occasionally to talk about our work and our lives. Since most of us were interested in improving teaching and learning, I originally called it the Education Development Discussion Group. Some members called it the Hunt Club, but very soon it became simply the Thursday Group.

We meet during the academic year on alternate Thursdays from 12:00 p.m. to 2:00 p.m. in a small classroom at OISE. The composition of the group changes slightly each year, numbering between twenty and twenty-five. We usually have about ten or twelve members attending, so we can comfortably sit around a large table. Members come from a wide variety of the helping professions — teachers, counsellors, nurses, consultants, and trainers — and usually about half of them are from OISE. Some members come from quite a distance to attend.

While originally we were a largely male, cigar-smoking group, these days we have more female members and smoking is forbidden. In the early days, I provided coffee and muffins. Later we organized ourselves to produce a book, *The Doctoral Thesis Journey: Reflections from Travelers and Guides* (1994), and the meager royalties paid for refreshments. These days, members bring their own snacks.

But some things have remained the same. First, we rarely have an agenda and in the rare instances where we do, it is something we have all agreed upon. For example, we occasionally invite a member to demonstrate his or her work through a mini-workshop. Second, we talk about our experiences, professional and personal, not about abstract theories or models. Occasionally an out-of-town visitor drops by and tries to describe an abstract academic model. In these instances we have to ask the visitor gently to describe their experience with the model, not the abstraction. We have held over three hundred Thursday Group meetings and I can't say that we have never discussed a theory or a model, but when we have done so, the discussion has grown out of our practical experience.

The Thursday Group is very important to me and I believe to many members. I often hear from alumni who have moved away, but call to find out if we are still meeting and send us their greetings. And when a former member returns, it is always cause for celebration. On several occasions, we have even acted as a support group for a colleague experiencing difficulty.

When I ask myself why the Thursday Group has continued to prosper over the years, I think it's because it exemplifies my belief in the importance of taking a lighthearted, open, and accepting approach. But equally important is our willingness to honour the mystery, which in this case is our willingness to come together to just be together. I know that when I come in on a Thursday, I feel myself relaxing in this aura of trust and goodwill.

I have no explicit aims in moderating the group, but I always try to provide an opportunity for members to discuss their present concerns. Perhaps it is this perpetual openness to the changing concerns of members over the years that contributes to its vitality. We still sometimes discuss members' professional activity and workshops, but we are just as likely these days to focus on health issues, what to do in retirement, and real estate. Whatever the topic, there is a special climate to our meetings. We want to listen to one another, we want to share our experience, we want to enjoy each other, and have fun. The result is the spontaneous and mysterious free flow of friendship that keeps us coming back.

Conclusion

To be a friend is part of being human. We become aware of our humanity at each step as we learn to be a friend. When we first become friends with ourselves, we depend on our human capacity for self-awareness. When we consider offering our friendship to others, we rely on our human ability to know and appreciate others. When we strengthen our friendship ties, we rely on our human capacity for imagination to create ties of trust and connection. Finally, when we devote ourselves completely to being a friend, we reveal our human capacity to develop and grow as we connect with our human potential.

Because I like to consolidate my thoughts into brief, succinct action guides, I will conclude with three suggestions to summarize the relationship between being a friend and being human.

1. **Begin with Ourselves.** Beginning with ourselves requires us to shift attention from the external world to looking within in order to discover our inner desires and fears, all of which help make us human. In learning about our own desires, we become aware of our personal need for friendship and how we can try to meet this need. Self-awareness also reveals our foibles, along with the realization that they are part of what makes us human. When we apply our insights about our own humanity to others, we are ready for the next step.

2. **Appreciate Everyone's Humanity.** We can appreciate the humanity of others by applying what we have learned about our own humanity. When we extend our awareness of our own desires, fears, and foibles to others, we realize that they possess these as well, that they are human like us.

3. **Imagine Our Possibilities.** Our imagination is one of our most powerful human possessions, as we discover when we imagine new ways for offering and

strengthening friendship. When we imagine our possibilities, we not only reveal new approaches to being a friend, but we discover our human capacity to release our human potential.

Finally, being a friend means accepting contradictions both within ourselves and, especially, between ourselves and others. Learning to be a friend is a lesson in learning how we are alike as human beings and how we are different in expressing our humanity. We are often drawn to others who are similar in belief, custom, and background, yet there is also great value in offering our friendship to those who are quite different. We can celebrate our humanity by offering our friendship to whomever we choose.

References

Dalai Lama. *Ancient Wisdom, Modern World: Ethics for the New Millennium*. London: Little Brown, 1999.

Heat-Moon, William Least. *Blue Highways: A Journey into America*. Boston: Little Brown, 1982.

Hunt, David E. *Beginning with Ourselves*. Cambridge, MA: Brookline Books, 1987.

_____. *The Renewal of Personal Energy*. Newbury Park, CA: Sage Publications, 1992.

_____. *Studies in Role Concept Repertory: Conceptual Consistency*. Unpublished Master's Thesis, Ohio State University, 1951.

Jarrett, Keith. "Liner Notes." *Keith Jarrett Trio at the Blue Note: The Complete Recording*. Munich: ECM, 1995.

Kelly, George A. *The Psychology of Personal Constructs. Volume 1*. New York: W.W. Norton, 1955.

Kluckhohn, Clyde and Henry A. Murray. *Personality in Nature, Society, and Culture*. New York: A.A. Knopf, 1948.

Kolb, David A. *Experiential Learning: Experience as the Source of Learning and Development*. Englewood Cliffs, NJ: Prentice Hall, 1984.

Moore, Thomas. *Soul Mates: Honoring the Mystery of Love and Relationships*. New York: Harper Perennial Publishers, 1994.

O'Donohue, John. *Anam Cara: A Book of Celtic Wisdom*. New York: HarperCollins, 1997.

Ornish Dean. *Dr. Dean Ornish's Program for Reversing Heart Disease: The Only System Scientifically Proven to Reverse Heart Disease Without Drugs or Surgery*. New York: Random House, 1990.

_____. *Love and Survival: The Scientific Basis for the Healing Power of Intimacy*. New York: HarperCollins, 1998.

Rilke, Rainer Maria. *Letters to a Young Poet*. New York: Random House, 1984.

Shield, Benjamin. "Letting Go of the Mountain." In *Handbook for the Soul*, edited by Richard Carlson and Benjamin Shield. New York: Back Bay Books, 1996.

Vanier, Jean. *Becoming Human*. Toronto: House of Anansi Press, 1998.

Journal Articles

Hunt, David E. "How to Be Your Own Best Theorist." *Theory into Practice*, 19, 87–293, 1980.

_____. "The New Three R's in Person-Environment Interaction: Responsiveness, Reciprocity, and Reflexivity." *Dutch Journal of Educational Research*, 14, 184–190, 1979.

_____. "Teachers' Adaptation: 'Reading' and 'Flexing' to Students." Journal *of Teacher Education*, 27, 268–275, 1976.

_____. "Teachers are Psychologists, Too: On the Application of Psychology to Education." *Canadian Psychological Review*, 17, 210–218, 1976.

Acknowledgements

I am grateful for all of the friendship I experienced during the ten years I worked on this book. The encouragement I received from family and friends kept me working through several earlier versions before completing this book in its current form. Before identifying specific individuals, I want to express my appreciation for several groups for their inspiration and support.

First, to all those participants in my earlier workshops for their willingness to begin with themselves. Their input from the workshop set the foundation and provided many examples for future workshops.

I also want to thank members of three important groups in my life: my Open Your Heart support group, my band, The Foolish Things, and my Thursday Group. I have learned a lot about friendship through my membership in these groups, and I deeply appreciate the friendship they provided.

There are many specific individuals I want to thank for their support and encouragement over the time I worked on this book. It has gone through four unpublished incarnations, and some individuals contributed to earlier versions, while a few persons have worked with me throughout the entire period. I appreciate the technical assistance from several computing consultants including Joseph Caprara, Tony Gallina, Tony Pitoschia, Allan Revich, and Michael Rosenthal. In the earlier versions, Heather Berkeley was a valuable partner in editing and offering suggestions, while Richard Tiberius's comments were an important source of encouragement.

I want to thank Mary Beattie for inviting me to participate in her research project, an experience that provided a valuable independent source of feedback for my work. As I worked on this final version, the suggestions of Jack Miller and Selia Karsten were extremely helpful. Evan Church offered encouragement and support throughout, and his example of opening his heart is an inspiration. Sheila Cook read and responded to each version, and offered valuable suggestions and support. Thanks to Marian Press and Seeta Nyary for their editorial assistance in early versions of this book. The final version is more accessibly thanks to the skillful work of my copy editor, Nicole Chaplin. I am I especially indebted to Malcolm Lester for his help in finding a publisher. Finally, and most of all, I am grateful for the ever present loving support from my wife, Jan.

About the Author

David E. Hunt is a psychologist who has been offering workshops and graduate courses on personal development for the past thirty years. He received his Ph.D. from Ohio State University, and taught at Yale and Syracuse before coming to the Ontario Institute for Studies in Education at the University of Toronto where he taught until his retirement in 2004. He has written several books, including *Beginning with Ourselves* and *The Renewal of Personal Energy*, which form the basis for his workshops on personal development and renewal. He is the recipient of the Canadian Education Association Award for Distinguished Contribution to Educational Research and the OCUFA Award for Outstanding Contribution to University Teaching. In 1986 he received an honourary Ph.D. from the University of Helsinki, and more recently, in 2003 he was honoured by the creation of a teaching award in his name to be awarded annually: the David E. Hunt Award for Excellence in Graduate Teaching.

Since retiring and completing this book, David Hunt is writing a memoir of his fifty years as a psychologist.

Of Related Interest

ACTS OF KINDESS
*Inspirational Stories
for Everyday Life*
edited by Adam Mayers
978-1554887491
$14.99

For the past five years readers of the *Toronto Star*'s website have sharing their stories in a feature called "Acts of Kindness." The common thread is that a stranger helped when it was needed most, without thought of a reward and often without leaving a name. Two hundred of the best stories featured in the *Star* are collected here. The stories are a reminder that goodness is non-denominational, non-political, and transferable across race and language. They also remind us that although our lives are full of hard realities, the smallest gesture can raise a spirit or lift a heart, and the time to do it is now.

THE TYRANNY OF NICENESS
Unmasking the Need for Approval
by Evelyn K. Sommers, Ph.D.
978-1550025583
$24.99

The Tyranny of Niceness identifies and confronts our most fundamental social dysfunction — niceness. For over fifteen years, Sommers, a Toronto psychologist, has treated many twisted lives created by being nice. She interweaves the case histories of her clients with her own observations to present a frightening, yet hopeful, picture of a society that promotes silence and obedience over individuality and honesty. Through her stories and analysis, we see that letting go of niceness, without being rude or uncivil, means a new way of relating to others and a new honesty with oneself.

What did you think of this book?

 **DUNDURN PRESS**
www.dundurn.com

Visit www.dundurn.com for reviews, videos, updates, and more!